Revised Edition

Should I
GET
MARRIED?

M. Blaine Smith

InterVarsity Press
Downers Grove, Illinois

*This book is dedicated
to my wife, Evie, and our sons,
Benjamin and Nathan,
who are a constant reminder to me
of God's grace
in creating families.*

InterVarsity Press
P.O. Box 1400, Downers Grove, IL 60515-1426
World Wide Web: www.ivpress.com
E-mail: mail@ivpress.com

First edition ©1990 by M. Blaine Smith
Revised edition ©2000 by M. Blaine Smith

InterVarsity Press® is the book-publishing division of InterVarsity Christian Fellowship/USA®, a student movement active on campus at hundreds of universities, colleges and schools of nursing in the United States of America, and a member movement of the International Fellowship of Evangelical Students. For information about local and regional activities, write Public Relations Dept., InterVarsity Christian Fellowship/USA, 6400 Schroeder Rd., P.O. Box 7895, Madison, WI 53707-7895.

All Scripture quotations, unless otherwise indicated, are taken from the Holy Bible, New International Version®. NIV®. *Copyright ©1973, 1978, 1984 by International Bible Society. Used by permission of Zondervan Publishing House. All rights reserved.*

The lyrics on p. 31 were written by Donna Walters and are used by permission.

Cover photograph: Michael Jang/Stone

ISBN 0-8308-2271-2

Printed in the United States of America ∞

Library of Congress Cataloging-in-Publication Data

Smith, M. Blaine.
  Should I get married? / M. Blaine Smith. —Rev. ed.
    p. cm.
  Includes bibliographical references.
  ISBN 0-8308-2271-2 (pbk. : alk. paper)
    1. Marriage —Religious aspects —Christianity. I. Title.

BV835 .S585 2000
248.4 —dc21

                                                                                  00-057505

18 17 16 15 14 13 12 11 10 9 8 7 6 5 4 3

14 13 12 11 10 09 08 07 06 05 04 03 02

Contents

Part One

Setting Your Sights

One

....

The Search for Perspective

MOST OF THE HAPPILY MARRIED COUPLES I KNOW CONFESS THAT the road to finding the right person was a rocky one at best. There were many false starts and disappointments along the way, and there was even a lot of confusion in reaching the decision they finally made. One very happily married woman in her late forties admitted to me in all honesty, "If I were widowed, I don't think I could go through the process of finding a husband again."

I do know a Christian couple who were acquainted only four days before becoming engaged. The decision to marry involved no struggle for either of them. Though only in their early twenties, they were both mature enough to make a wise choice. They've been married over twenty-five years now and have had an excellent relationship. They show that whatever may be said about the difficulty of choosing a marriage partner or the need for a long acquaintance period, there are exceptions to every rule.

I'm hard pressed, though, to think of another example like theirs. My own odyssey toward marriage definitely fit the rule and not the exception. I was painfully shy as an adolescent and teenager. While I did enjoy a dating relationship in my young teens that lasted over a year, several others which I longed to initiate never got off the ground. Things began to improve after I gave my life to Christ at age nineteen. My social confidence in general increased remarkably.

By the time I was twenty-five, however, I'd been through three relationships where my expectations were seriously disappointed. In one I even believed I'd received a revelation from God that we would marry—something that in time proved to be just wishful thinking. In another, all the signposts seemed to indicate marriage, and we enjoyed a good relationship for a year and a half. Yet in time we discovered our vocational goals were so different that they made marriage untenable. Following a seminar that left me guilt-ridden for wanting marriage so much, I even resolved to forsake dating for a semester. While some important benefits came from this time, I realize now that my motives for this temporary vow of singleness were less than healthy.

Things took a very encouraging turn when I was twenty-six and began dating Evie Kirkland. We were married within a year! In the end God's grace triumphed over my own blundering and confusion as it always does. Yet I must confess I felt like a ship lost at sea without a compass for much of this time. I know that much of my pain and poor judgment could have been eliminated if I'd had better instruction on how to choose a life partner.

Some Common Concerns

So many Christian singles have told me they are frustrated or confused in dealing with relationships and the question of marriage that I'm certain my own experience with deciding to marry is the rule and not the exception today. There are several points at which many feel adrift.

Married or single? Some are stuck at how to resolve the basic choice between marriage and singleness. We who are married can quickly forget what a complicated question this is for many singles, who hear different ideals about marriage and singleness being tossed around. Should you follow one of these ideals—and

if so, which one—or is it okay to simply follow your own preference? How do you find God's will in the midst of it all?

Getting off square one. Many others are quite comfortable with
the idea of being married yet just as uncertain about how to get
there. I know many bright, likeable singles well into their adult
years who deeply want to be married but for various reasons are
not. A surprising number have never had a serious dating relationship at all.

Making the choice. Perhaps most surprising is how many are in
serious relationships yet unable to resolve whether to marry. The
majority of those seeking my counsel in recent years, in fact,
have been looking for advice about whether to marry a particular person. Many of these are mature Christians with long-stand-
ing relationships in which one or both cannot decide about
marriage. In some cases the concern is over needing a clear sign
from God. In others it's over whether one's ideals can be fully
met in the relationship.

The fear of commitment. Still, some hesitate to marry from fears
that marriage itself may be an overly confining or unpleasant experience. Not a few speak of commitment as claustrophobic—
like being stuck in an elevator. A mature Christian woman admitted to me recently: "You know, I long for a relationship with a
man, but when it finally becomes apparent that he wants to get
serious I panic and want out. Once the relationship is over and
the threat of commitment gone, I start liking him again." The
fear of commitment causes some to bail out of perfectly good relationships and others to avoid dating altogether.

A map for the journey ahead. Finally, there are many who, while
not overly concerned about getting married at this point, would
like some perspective on how to move toward marriage at some
time in the future. Too often they end up frustrated, for little
meaningful direction on this matter is given by the church today.
Among the many churches with which I'm acquainted, few offer
any teaching on finding or choosing a spouse. And while several
books on the subject did emerge during the 1990s, helpful books

for the Christian on the marriage decision still remain few and far between.

Encouragement and Direction

That brings me to the purpose of this book. I wrote it to give navigational direction to those who are at each of these points of need, and to offer spiritual encouragement as well. This is a guidebook for working through the major stages in considering marriage. My interest has been fueled especially by remembering how helpful it would have been for me to have a volume of this sort available as a young believer.

This is a revised edition of *Should I Get Married?* which has been in print now for ten years. I've provided additional counsel and examples in various places. I've also added several major sections which I'll note in a moment. I've focused my concern in this new edition more exclusively on how to make a wise choice of whom you marry. I address my counsel to those who are in a serious relationship or considering one, to help them determine whether marriage is the right step. I've removed a section that was in the first edition on finding a spouse, in order to allow more space for the book's primary concern.

If you have picked up this book for help in finding someone to marry, you can still benefit significantly from the book's material, and I would encourage you to read what follows carefully. Determining what it is you are looking for in a relationship is a vital step toward finding one. I find time and again that singles who are eager for marriage often are harboring unrealistic ideals that are hindering them from finding someone who is truly suitable for them.

In fact, clarifying your expectations can simplify the search for a mate, sometimes considerably. Some even find that they already know someone who would make an excellent spouse — perhaps a close friend — whom they've overlooked because their expectations were unreasonable. While this may or may not be true in your case, be open to that possibility as you read.

Three Blind Spots

When I reflect on my experience as a single Christian, I'm struck by two things. First, I'm certain that some of the difficulties I experienced were unavoidable. There is a mystery—in short, a risk—in human relationships that can never be avoided if we are to experience the adventure of life as God has designed it and move toward the goal of an intimate lifetime relationship.

Yet I also realize only too well that some of my problems resulted from certain well-intentioned but misguided perspectives which made me prone to bad judgment and a sitting duck for disappointment. In my work with singles today I find these same unfortunate viewpoints coming up again and again, and the problems that result are all too predictable. They tend to fall under three general areas:

One is *spiritualizing*. By "spiritualizing" I mean expecting an unreasonable measure of guidance from God. Scripture shows that while God graciously guides our decisions, he seldom eliminates the need for us to think them through and ultimately take responsibility for resolving them. Yet many Christians expect him to guide in a mystical or supernatural fashion which would supersede this process and remove all personal responsibility.

Such a belief leaves some Christians uneasy about taking any personal initiative in finding a marriage partner. Others who are in serious relationships feel compelled to wait for an unmistakable sign from God before finally deciding to marry. And some are too quick to think God has given them a revelation to marry through some inner feeling or ironic coincidence. They don't do the hard work of carefully thinking the decision through.

Similar problems are caused by *idealizing*. We may hold to unreasonable ideals about romantic love or the perfect mate. Having ideals for marriage is crucial, but it is vital that these be realistic and in line with God's best intentions for our life. In reality the influence of both our secular and Christian cultures is such that few of us enter adulthood without the need for some—often drastic—revising of our ideals before we will be in a position to find a suitable mate or make healthy decisions about marriage.

Many fail to see the marriage potential in a good relationship because their partner (or their feeling of romantic love) falls short of some unreasonable ideal. Others are too quick to think they have found the perfect companion in someone who seems to match up to certain stereotypes.

A third mindset that can be just as great an obstacle to sound decision making is *catastrophizing.* By this term I mean harboring unreasonable fears of risk or change by dwelling on problems that are not likely to occur, or obsessing over the possibility of making a wrong decision. A variety of normal fears arise as we take steps toward marriage, ranging from the fear of rejection to the fear of decision making to the fear of commitment itself. The fear of commitment is the one which most typically hinders those in good relationships from going ahead with marriage.

Some fear is healthy in a step as major as marriage, for it causes you to take the decision seriously and spurs you to trust more fully in Christ. But excessive fear can hinder clear thinking about marriage and keep you from going ahead when a suitable opportunity presents itself. Without some willingness to risk, indeed without a proper sense of adventure, you will never take the plunge into marriage.

Throughout the book I'll look at misleading ideas that arise in each of these three areas and how they can get you off track in considering marriage. I'll draw on examples from my own life and the experiences of others whom I've known and counseled. At each point I'll do my best to point you to outlooks which I understand to be more in line with Scripture and healthy thinking. My hope is that this book will benefit you in three major ways:

☐ By helping you clarify how Christ's responsibility and your own relate in decisions about marriage.

☐ By helping you establish healthy ideals about marriage, singleness and whom you would consider marrying.

☐ By giving you perspective on how to deal with fears that may be keeping you from God's best in these areas, particularly the fear of commitment. (I've authored another book specifically on the fear of rejection, *Overcoming Shyness*,[1] and I encourage you to read it if this is an area where you need special help.)

Our Task Ahead

We will begin by looking at the question of choosing between marriage and singleness (chapter two). Because this is foundational to everything else considered in this book, I want to begin by offering clear counsel for thinking this issue through.

In part two we will take a close look at God's guidance in our lives, especially as it touches decisions related to marriage. While I stress God's role in finding a spouse and the vital need for faith and trust on our part, I also examine some common misconceptions about how the Lord guides our decisions—misconceptions that can keep you from taking proper responsibility for finding a mate or from clear thinking when it comes to making a decision about marrying someone.

Part three is the heart of the book. It provides perspective for deciding whether to marry once you're in a serious relationship. I offer guidelines for assessing your compatibility with another person, your readiness for marriage and whether the balance of factors adds up to a decision for marriage.

In part four I offer counsel and encouragement to divorced persons considering remarriage and to those considering marrying someone divorced, and I look at biblical and practical issues involved. This material is new to this edition of *Should I Get Married?*; I did not deal with remarriage in the first edition at all.

In part five I examine the fear of commitment, looking at problems it causes and how to deal with them. I discuss how to recognize this fear in yourself or someone else, how to respond to someone who is afraid of commitment and, if this fear is a problem for you personally, what steps you can take to overcome it. I've given considerable attention to this area during the past ten years and have published a book devoted to it—*The Yes Anxi-*

ety.[2] I've grown more optimistic about the possibility of one's overcoming commitment fear and offer much more counsel related to healing than I did in the first edition of this book.

I have also added an appendix on the question of whether Christian singles should date. While this was rarely an issue ten years ago, it is a major one for many singles today, due especially to the popularity of Joshua Harris's *I Kissed Dating Goodbye*, published in 1997. The question is a challenging one now for many considering marrying someone or beginning a serious relationship. In appendix one I explore the issues related to it and suggest how to determine whether a dating or nondating approach to courtship is best for you personally.

Finally, I've added "Vows for the Imperfect Marriage" (appendix two). These are simply a few statements that reflect the theme of this book: that God provides us with a most suitable but imperfect partner—and that two imperfect human beings can realistically have a marriage filled with understanding, forgiveness and love.

While I cite many real-life incidents throughout the book, I've changed names and incidental details in some cases in order to protect the identities of those involved. I've also felt free to combine and create examples to illustrate particular points.

Staying Hopeful

Finally, let me mention that my experience gives me not only empathy for the struggles of single Christians but an important basis for extending hope as well. For one thing, my ministry has brought me into contact with many who are truly contented and joyful in the single life. I've seen many times the grace and fullness of life that God gives to those who are single. If you are single, I hope you will take considerable encouragement from the discussion ahead.

I've often been impressed, too, with how God can work miracles to bring two people together in a lifetime union. I share the awe of a couple I married, who felt it remarkable that they grew up three thousand miles apart, in radically different circumstances, yet through the providence of God met and decided to marry.

My own experience as a single Christian taught me the significance of certain changes in perspective, and this more than anything inspired me to write this book. As my thinking changed at several important points, my journey toward marriage progressed as well. The result has been twenty-seven years of a happy, fulfilling marriage. I've seen this pattern repeated time and again for many who at one point were ready to give up but now are in happy, solid marriages.

I say this cautiously, for—in spite of the preposterous claims of some popular titles—no book can guarantee that you will find a marriage partner. Yet I'm confident that the perspectives presented here can improve your prospects—perhaps considerably—and help you be more fully open to the abundant provision of Christ for your life.

My strongest conviction is that these perspectives will help you make a wise choice and move into marriage with confidence once the right opportunity presents itself.

In short, I write this book in a highly optimistic and hopeful spirit. I hope that spirit will be contagious in the pages ahead.

Two

Does God Want Me to Be Married or Single?

HAS GOD CREATED ME TO BE A MARRIED PERSON, OR AM I BETTER suited for staying single? In which state will I be most fulfilled? In which will I best serve Christ? How can I know which is God's will for me?

Before we can talk about principles for choosing a mate or guidelines for building a serious relationship, we need first to consider the more fundamental question of choosing between marriage and single life. The question is important not only for those who are unattached and wondering how to direct their energies but also for those in serious relationships who are confused about whether to forsake the single life for marriage.

Fortunately, Scripture speaks to this issue in a clear and liberating way. Unfortunately, this is an area where Christians are especially prone to unhealthy idealizing. The balanced message of Scripture is often overshadowed by idealized perspectives which are assumed to be biblical. This idealizing is at the root of most of the confusion that Christians experience in choosing between marriage and the single life. It happens in three common ways.

Married or Buried
Some Christians idealize marriage. Some even go so far as to re-

gard it as an almost universal need. Though it's seldom said explicitly, there is an underlying assumption in many churches and Christian groups that marriage is a more healthy state than singleness. While this view creates a comfortable climate for those who want to pursue marriage, it wreaks havoc for those who either cannot find a mate or wish to remain unattached.

In *Single and Whole* Rhena Taylor documents her struggle to accept herself as a single woman among friends who feel she is missing something essential to life. Rhena is a contented single. As an energetic and creative missionary, she enjoys the freedom of being unattached. No matter how deeply she looks into herself, she cannot find a gaping need waiting to be filled by a husband and family.

Yet friends console her for being without a mate. They read feelings into her that simply aren't there. They tell her in subtle or not so subtle ways that she would be happier and more effective married. Perhaps worst of all, she notes, "In over thirty years now as a Christian, I have never heard a minister of God preach on singleness as a good option for a Christian. I have sat through sermon after sermon after sermon on marriage, but I have never heard a recommendation for the single state even though the pews have been filled with single people."[1]

There is no question that many Christians overglamorize marriage. In many Christian circles those who opt for singleness do so at the cost of being regarded as second-class citizens. Others who are well suited for single life are unfairly pressured toward marriage.

Bachelors till the Rapture

The problem, though, is often as great in the other direction. While some Christians idealize marriage, others exalt singleness. While no one would suggest that God wants all Christians to be single, there's a tendency in some Christian circles to think of the single life as a more virtuous state than the married.

Churches and parachurch ministries that place a high premium on missionary service often stress the special advantages of freedom which a single person has for such work. While some do this with a healthy sense of balance, others come off saying that the single person is actually in a better position than the married one to serve the Lord as a missionary.

Singles ministries, seminars and books stress the benefits of singleness not only for those in missionary service but for Christians in all walks of life. Again, while some do this with a proper respect for individual gifts and callings, others imply that the single person in general is following a higher calling than the one who settles for marriage.

Those who idealize the single life cite compelling biblical evidence for their position. Jesus and Paul, the two most significant personalities in the New Testament, were both single. And Paul spoke expressly of the benefits of the single life for devotion and service to the Lord. In 1 Corinthians 7:32-34 we read:

> I would like you to be free from concern. An unmarried man is concerned about the Lord's affairs—how he can please the Lord. But a married man is concerned about the affairs of this world— how he can please his wife—and his interests are divided. An unmarried woman or virgin is concerned about the Lord's affairs: Her aim is to be devoted to the Lord in both body and spirit. But a married woman is concerned about the affairs of this world—how she can please her husband.

There is no question that Paul saw special advantages in staying single. Yet these words must be understood in the context of other statements Paul made which bring balance to his perspective.[2]

Some Christians, like Rhena Taylor, are contented in the single state and enjoy the special benefits of being unattached. Like anyone, they go through periods of loneliness. Yet generally they are not preoccupied with thoughts of marriage and longings for a partner. They truly reflect the joyful single state that Paul talks about.

Some, though, who regard singleness as a higher calling, find it hard to bring their desires up to the level of their ideals. Underneath, they would strongly prefer to be married. If they do marry, they are nagged with the fear that they have settled for a less perfect will of God than they otherwise could have known. If they stay single, they consume a lot of energy dreaming about what marriage would be like. This often leads to self-deprecation and guilt for not being contented with God's "ideal," and the problem is compounded.

I Don't Deserve to Be Married

There's another reason why Christians opt for singleness, though, which has little to do with a high regard for the single life. Some regard marriage as a prize so high that they assume they couldn't possibly be worthy of it. They look upon marriage as a reward which God gives to those who merit it through living an exemplary Christian life—a merit they personally could never achieve.

While this may seem a surprising viewpoint to those who don't identify with it, a number of serious Christians fall into it. They may believe that their behavior in past dating relationships or their fantasies about sex have been too ungodly to merit God's gift of marriage. Staying single becomes a form of self-punishment, a way of atoning for their own sins.

If those who think this way do marry, they may either be dogged with guilt or feel an unhealthy pride in having merited the "reward" of marriage. Sometimes, too, they hold a scrupulously high moral standard for the person they would consider marrying and are unforgiving of failings.

The Biblical Perspective

Each of these idealized perspectives carries an element of biblical truth: God *does* will that most Christians eventually marry. Singleness *does* confer special advantages of grace for certain individuals. Marriage *is* an extraordinary gift of God.

Yet each of these positions errs in taking the truth to an unhealthy extreme. There is no basis in Scripture for regarding either marriage or singleness as a more noble state in itself—it's always a question of God's will for an individual. And while marriage is a bountiful gift, it's never regarded in Scripture as a reward which one must merit.

When the biblical perspective on marriage and singleness is fully understood, it is found to be both balanced and liberating. It at once avoids the idealizing of the popular perspectives and gives us a succinct basis for deciding what our life's orientation should be. Perhaps most surprisingly, it puts the emphasis upon *personal preference* as the key to understanding God's will.

To summarize the biblical perspective:

1. Marriage is given not because we deserve it but because we need it. Scripture teaches that marriage, like salvation itself, is an unmerited gift from God. In the first reference to marriage in Scripture we read: "The LORD God said, 'It is not good for the man to be alone. I will make a helper suitable for him' " (Gen 2:18). Only one reason is mentioned for God's bringing Eve into Adam's life—the fact that Adam needed companionship. Nothing is said about Adam deserving a wife, nor is it even suggested that Adam would serve God better with a spouse. It's simply said that Adam had a personal need, and this was basis enough for God to fill the void.

Several verses later it becomes clear that Adam and Eve reflect God's intentions for humanity in general. "For this reason a man will leave his father and mother and be united to his wife, and they will become one flesh" (Gen 2:24). Just as Adam and Eve were brought together because of their mutual need, so God deems that others will be led by their own companionship needs to seek a spouse.

Paul reiterates the point in 1 Corinthians 7:1-6, in light of our inherent need for sexual fulfillment. One would have to read this passage with blinders on to miss its explicit message:

> Now for the matters you wrote about: It is good for a man not to marry. But since there is so much immorality, each man should have his own wife, and each woman her own husband. The husband should fulfill his marital duty to his wife, and likewise the wife to her husband. The wife's body does not belong to her alone

but also to her husband. In the same way, the husband's body does not belong to him alone but also to his wife. Do not deprive each other except by mutual consent and for a time, so that you may devote yourselves to prayer. Then come together again so that Satan will not tempt you because of your lack of self-control. I say this as a concession, not as a command.

Then Paul goes on (v. 7 NRSV) to point out:

I wish that all were as I myself am. But each has a particular gift from God, one having one kind and another a different kind.

In graphic language Paul says that marriage is a gift to help us avoid the inclination toward sexual immorality. Our idealistic mindset would expect Paul to say, "Since there is so much immorality, you must first prove yourself morally worthy to be married." Or, "Since there is so much immorality, you must avoid marriage, since it would indulge your sexual appetite." But to the contrary, Paul sees marriage as an *antidote* to sexual impurity.

Paul puts aside the philosophy which says that marriage is a reward for personal righteousness. To those who hold that philosophy, Paul would say: "Yes, you're correct in saying you don't deserve to be married. Who deserves any of God's gifts? Yet you may well *need* to be married. If you do, and you have a suitable opportunity, you will better honor Christ by marrying. To choose not to marry in this instance would amount to choosing to live the Christian life through your own strength rather than accepting God's provision of grace."

2. Celibacy is a gift given to some but not all. Paul's language clearly indicates that most Christians will best serve Christ through getting married: "Each man should have his own wife, and each woman her own husband." But Paul stops far short of the popular philosophy that idealizes marriage and views it as a universal need. He also extols the benefits of the single life, beginning 1 Corinthians 7 with the statement "It is good for a man not to marry," then referring to his own enjoyment of the single life (v. 7), and finally noting explicitly how being single frees you from certain burdens that inevitably come from being married (vv. 32-35).

Crucial to understanding Paul's perspective on singleness, though, is the fact that he regards the ability to live contentedly unmarried as *a spiritual gift*. "Each has a particular gift from God, one having one kind and another a different kind" (v. 7 NRSV). In 1 Corinthians 12 Paul compares spiritual gifts to parts of the human body. Through this supremely helpful metaphor Paul shows that either you have a particular spiritual gift or you don't. You cannot gain a gift just by wishing for it any more than a toe can become an eye.

This analogy also suggests that it's not difficult to know whether you have a certain gift. Just as you realize without effort that you have hands and feet, so the presence of a spiritual gift is obvious.

In his classic *Your Spiritual Gifts Can Help Your Church Grow*, C. Peter Wagner offers straightforward advice on how to recognize if you have the gift of singleness:

> If you are single and know down in your heart that you would get married in an instant if a reasonable opportunity presented itself, you probably don't have the gift [of singleness]. If you are single and find yourself terribly frustrated by unfulfilled sexual impulses, you probably don't have the gift. But if neither of these things seems to bother you, rejoice—you may have found one of your spiritual gifts.[3]

I heartily concur with Wagner's counsel. Discovering whether God wants you to set your heart on staying single is usually as simple a matter as discerning what it really is you want to do.

This isn't to say that you can't be chaste and fulfilled as a single person even though you lack the gift of singleness. God will give you all the power needed to stay pure and to enjoy life even though your desire for marriage remains unfulfilled. Yet it will require a measure of discipline and conscious drawing on God's grace which the one with the gift of singleness doesn't have to be concerned with. For that person being single is natural. It requires no heroic discipline.

The Bottom Line

What we're saying, then, boils down to several implications:

☐ If you want to be married, you should feel free to stay open to the possibility. You don't have to trouble yourself with thoughts like "What if God really wants me to plan on staying single?" Of course, the final proof that God wants you married will be his making it possible. It would be wrong to think that your desire for marriage is a prophetic indication that God will definitely provide you a mate. Time alone will tell that. But it would be just as wrong to think that he might be expecting you to plan to stay forever single or to take a perpetual vow of celibacy. You are free to stay open and hopeful about the possibility of marriage.

☐ If, on the other hand, you know that you'd prefer to stay single, then you don't have to trouble yourself with the thought *What if God really wants me to be married?* Nor do you have to think of yourself as a second-class citizen of the kingdom of God. You can relax, enjoy the extraordinary gift of singleness God has given you and look for the best ways to invest your life as a single person. And those friends who keep urging you to seek marriage? You can tell them (sensitively, of course) to get off your back.

☐ But what if you're on the fence? You're not certain if you want to marry or stay single. In the first edition of this book I gave simple counsel in this case: just relax, and let the answer emerge in time. This seemed the logical and reverent answer to not being sure.

Then, at a seminar I gave, two women—friends who were attending together—took me to task for this advice. They explained that they were single, in their mid-thirties, and just now waking up to the fact that they wanted to be married. They regretted that they had sunk so much of their lives into their careers up to this point and hadn't clearly faced up sooner to their desire to marry. They felt they had lost valuable time that they should have invested in preparing for marriage and in finding a partner.

Their response convinced me that my counsel on this issue *was* too simplistic. There are some fortunate individuals who are equally and perpetually happy being either single or married. If you are confident that you fit this description, then my original advice holds: don't feel under any constraint to resolve the question. If marriage comes along, fine; if not, fine. It's a win-win situation either way. Yet not everyone is wired this way.

There are many, like the two women at my seminar, who live for some time with uncertainty about marriage, but then their biological clock gives them a wake-up call. They realize they do want to be married and regret they haven't focused more on that need before. In this case the desire for marriage usually has been underlying, but they haven't fully recognized it.

How can we fail to perceive an underlying desire for marriage? We may be so caught up in our career that we put off dealing with the question beyond a reasonable point. Fears may hinder us from facing it—ranging from the fear of rejection to the fear of commitment to an inordinate fear of ending up in a bad marriage. And, as we've noted, idealizing about singleness in Christian circles may discourage us from being honest with ourselves and others about our desire to marry.

If any of these shoes fit, I would encourage you to take the time and make the effort to clarify your feelings about marriage and singleness. You may sell yourself short by not doing so. We are much more likely to accomplish a desire when we recognize it and own it than when it's only a vague ambition. When a desire becomes specific—and especially when it becomes a goal—we more naturally do those things and give those signals to others that help us achieve our purpose.

Read the remainder of this book with an eye to resolving the question of whether you wish to be married or single. You may find it beneficial as well to explore the issue with a counselor or to take a personal retreat to focus on it. Don't be afraid to face your desire for marriage head-on, if this really is what underneath you want to do—or to acknowledge the desire to remain single, if that truly reflects your inner self.

Addicted to Dating?

At a different extreme, some singles enjoy dating so much that they allow it to be almost a substitute for marriage. I'm not against dating at all, and in fact I regard it as a beneficial process for many—if not most—of us in finding a mate (see appendix one for a detailed discussion). Yet I don't believe that God ever intended dating to be a *substitute* for marriage.

Some popular singles prefer the exhilaration of new relationships to the stability of a permanent one, and they bounce endlessly from one short-term relationship to another. Others allow themselves enough sexual liberty within dating that they prefer the uncommitted environment of dating as a sexual outlet rather than marriage with its other responsibilities.

If either of these situations describes your life, do yourself a favor. Realize that your great enjoyment of dating demonstrates that you really need to be married and that God has created you with this need; 1 Corinthians 7 couldn't be clearer on this point. Recognize also that by letting dating function as a substitute for marriage, you are living well short of God's ideal and missing some of his greatest blessings.

Chances are very good, too, that you are too idealistic about the person whom you would consider marrying.

May I say it lovingly? It's time to grow up. Develop a perspective on marriage and choosing a mate that's right for you—and that is *achievable.* Read the pages ahead for direction. Explore the issue with a pastor, competent counselor or trusted friend. Let go of any thought that the person you marry must be perfect. Make it your goal to find someone to marry who is suitable for you. And pray for God's grace and wisdom to resolve this matter within a reasonable time.

Is There a Time to Let Go of Your Hope for Marriage?

A remaining question is whether you reach a point, with the passing of years or after a number of failed relationships, where you should conclude that God has shown you through the force of circumstances that he doesn't want you ever to marry. Does the time finally come when you should let go of the desire to marry and set your heart on staying perpetually single?

I want to say emphatically that you never *have to* conclude that God has told you he never wants you to marry or that he has permanently shut the door. It may be that (a) you decide you would really prefer to stay single or (b) God gives you an unusual, supernatural revelation that you should not marry. Apart from either of these occurrences you are not compelled to let go of your hope.

Even a superficial reading of Scripture shows that God has radically different timetables for his children. Some realize important goals early in life, others at later points. This applies as much to the area of finding a mate as to any other. I have seen such encouraging examples, including a woman I know who married for the first time at age fifty and, just recently, another female friend who became engaged for the first time at age sixty-nine—and it was her first dating relationship ever. In *Singles, Sex and Marriage* Herbert J. Miles gives the heartening example and testimony of a woman who was sixty at the time of marriage—his own wife.[4] It was her first marriage and the second for Miles, a widower.

I mention these merely as examples; I don't believe there's any upper age limit when you must conclude, "It is now too late for me."

I realize it can be extremely disheartening to move into your later twenties, thirties or perhaps well beyond, wanting to be married but not finding a suitable prospect. I don't mean to minimize the pain involved here at all. Some feel they must give up on their search for marriage and resolve to stay single simply to preserve their mental health. Before you do that, though, let me urge you to read the remainder of this book. It may be that changing your perspective in certain ways will make your search for a spouse more fruitful.

In the meantime don't give up on yourself. And remember that Scripture reminds us again and again that prayer and perseverance in our efforts eventually bear fruit. Remember too that God is not your adversary but your friend, who desires the absolute best for your life. That alone is reason for staying hopeful.

Part Two

God's Guidance &
the Marriage Decision

Three

· · · · · · · · · · ·

Does God Have
One Ideal Choice for Me?

A MEMBER OF THE CHURCH I ATTENDED AS A SINGLE CHRISTIAN
wrote a song that became a favorite at weddings held there.
Many couples began their wedding ceremonies with it, and Evie
and I used it as the invocation for our own service. The first
verse sets forth the theme that continues throughout the song:

> Long, long ago, before God gave us life,
> Before our souls had substance,
> Before our eyes could see,
> He planned us for each other,
> Each one for the other,
> He planned that this day would come to be.[1]

The song proclaims a belief which Christians have long held
sacred—that God predetermines whom you marry. If he wants
you to be married, there is one ideal choice in his mind for you.
And he works in many mysterious ways to bring you to the one
for whom you are destined.

Writing this book challenged me to think back to our decision
to include that song in our wedding service and to wonder if—
beautiful as the song was—it was the wisest and most sensitive
choice we could have made. Do I still hold to its premise as

strongly as I did then? And was it edifying to proclaim it to others with trumpets as we did in our ceremony?

I have no question that some Christians benefit from the belief that God predestines your spouse. It inspires many married couples to view their relationship as more than a chance occurrence and to appreciate the hand of God in bringing them together. This leads to deeper reverence for Christ and greater faithfulness in their marriage. Many who are single, too, take heart in the thought that if God wants them to be married, he will move mountains to make it happen. They are inspired to stay hopeful and to take the sometimes scary steps needed to find a spouse.

Yet I find that just as frequently this viewpoint has an adverse effect on Christians. Some who are married feel an unhealthy sense of superiority over single friends for having been handpicked by God for the estate of marriage. Others are too quick to blame God for problems that come up in their marriage (see, for example, Gen 3:12).

Most unfortunate, though, is the paralyzing effect this notion sometimes has on single Christians who want to be married. Some conclude that any personal effort to find a spouse is outside the bounds of faith. Changing jobs or churches to improve the prospects of meeting someone compatible, for instance, is out of the question. Faith demands that you sit still and wait for God to bring the right person to your doorstep.

In one extreme case a Christian woman told me she felt she must avoid any situation that would make it too easy to find a husband. She had four opportunities for missionary service. In three of these situations there were single men whom she might consider marrying. Thus she felt compelled to choose the fourth. Though this woman, who was past forty, deeply wanted to be married, she greatly feared getting her own will mixed up with God's in the matter. Making it as difficult as possible for God to bring a man into her life would help ensure that marriage would come about only if God willed.

The belief that God has one ideal choice also leads some to be too idealistic about whom they would consider marrying. Since God is perfect, it is felt that you must not settle for anyone who less than fully measures up to your image of the ideal mate. Such persons are quick to bail out of a relationship at the first sign of another's imperfections, while others wait endlessly for that perfect relationship that never comes along.

Not Going Beyond Scripture

I must confess I wince a bit when I remember how Evie and I included the song about God predestining us in our ceremony without considering the effect its message might have on others. I fear, too, that there was something too smug or self-congratulatory in our desire to announce to the world that God had determined from before time to bring us together. I shudder when I think that several other couples who featured this same song in their weddings are now divorced. We certainly tread on thin ice whenever we declare unreservedly that we know particulars of God's hidden plan for our lives.

It's not that I'm ready to reject the premise of the song. My Presbyterian background has given me profound respect for the extensive biblical teaching on God's sovereignty and has taught me to be at home with paradox in the Christian life. I'm comfortable with the thought that God can give us full freedom to choose and act on the human level, yet still on a deeper, more mysterious level be ordering what we do in light of a preconceived plan.

My experience, though, is that most Christians do not find this notion helpful when it comes to decisions related to marriage. In an area as deeply personal, life-changing and far-reaching as moving toward marriage, it is vital that we be guided by the most clear and obvious teachings of Scripture and guard against getting sidetracked by speculative notions. Certainly God has told us what he wants us to know clearly and straightforwardly.

Here it is striking that Scripture never specifically states that God predestines a man and woman for each other in marriage. Even though this belief was deeply embedded in Jewish tradition and reflected in a number of sayings and anecdotes in the Talmud, the Holy Spirit did not choose to state matters so specifically in the inspired Scripture. This suggests that, whether or not there is truth in the notion, it is not an edifying one for most believers to keep in mind as they take steps toward marriage. This isn't to imply that Scripture has nothing to say about God's role in bringing about marriage. Quite the contrary! But the Bible in general views the responsibility as a *cooperative* one, where both God and we play a part in the process. This is a most liberating concept when it is fully appreciated, but a challenging one as well. To this end Scripture stresses three perspectives which are important to keep in mind.

The Call to Optimism

You have supreme basis for optimism as you seek to find a life partner. While Scripture does not directly address the question of whether God predestines a specific man and woman for each other, it does indicate that he gives a special measure of guidance and help—and very often success—to those who seek the opportunity for marriage.

When Paul, for instance, encourages Christians who need to be married to get married, he shows a remarkable confidence that those seeking a partner will be able to find one. In declaring "let each man have his own wife and each woman her own husband" (1 Cor 7:2 NEB), he doesn't even entertain the possibility that someone needing marriage will be unable to find an acceptable partner! His optimism is especially intriguing when we remember who he is addressing—a fledgling Christian community barely five years old where the pool of qualified candidates for marriage was surely not vast. Yet Paul's outlook is fueled by faith in a God whose hand is not shortened when it comes to meeting the needs of his saints.

Paul begins his letter to the Corinthians with a declaration of confidence that God will sustain them and meet the deepest needs in their lives:

I always thank God for you because of his grace given you in

Christ Jesus. For in him you have been enriched in every way. . . . Therefore you do not lack any spiritual gift as you eagerly wait for our Lord Jesus Christ to be revealed. He will keep you strong to the end, so that you will be blameless on the day of our Lord Jesus Christ. God, who has called you into fellowship with his Son Jesus Christ our Lord, is faithful. (1 Cor 1:4-5, 7-9)

This faith in Christ's provision for the Corinthians' needs undergirds all of Paul's remarks in his letter to the young church. He writes with the underlying confidence that as they seek to make intelligent choices, God will work for good in their lives.

To be sure, Paul stops short of guaranteeing that God will provide a spouse to anyone who wants one. Neither here nor anywhere else does Paul or any biblical writer lock God into a required response to any human need. There is always the possibility that God will choose not to meet a need directly but to give the grace to live contentedly with unfulfilled desires, a point Paul stresses in his second letter to this church (2 Cor 12:7-10).

Still Paul puts the accent on hope in his teaching on marriage, and throughout his writings he urges us toward faith in a God who provides all of our needs in Jesus Christ (Phil 4:19). If you want to be married, you certainly have reason to stay hopeful that God will provide someone to meet that need unless he changes your desire or in some clear way shuts the door.

Again, it is important as you maintain this hope to keep your expectations within reasonable bounds. If you're thinking, "God has one ideal choice for me," you may be setting your standards for that person impossibly high. When we consider the perspective on God's role which was in Paul's mind as he wrote 1 Corinthians 7, it seems to be not "God has one ideal person for you to marry" but "God will help you find a *suitable* partner." This is usually a more edifying thought to dwell on. The person whom he gives you to marry will have imperfections and failings, just as you do. Still that person will complement you in a way that will work for your greater happiness and a more fruitful life together for Christ.

The Call to Responsibility

At a party one evening, when this book was in process, I got to talking with a married friend about it. Our conversation wandered onto the question of how faith and personal responsibility work together in finding a spouse. At that moment her husband walked by, and she handed him an empty glass and asked him to fill it with ice for her. I remarked jokingly: "If your faith were strong enough, Molly, your husband would have known you wanted the glass filled without your asking. In fact, if your faith were *really* strong enough, you would have just held the glass out and the ice would have plopped into it!"

She replied: "But isn't this exactly how many Christians are thinking when it comes to finding a partner for marriage? You simply hold the glass out and the ice drops in."

She is right. When we talk about faith, some are left thinking that the burden is completely upon God to bring results. They think that we have no responsibility for the outcome.

Scripture, though, never views matchmaking this way. It always sees it as a mutual process where both God and the one wanting marriage have responsibility for the outcome. It involves not only waiting in faith but taking steps of faith as well.

Thus Paul speaks in 1 Thessalonians 4:4 about the attitude in which a man should "take" a wife, using a verb that implies personal initiative.[2] And in his whole discussion of the importance of marriage in 1 Corinthians 7, he says nothing about waiting passively for God to provide a spouse. Rather, he speaks to individual initiative in saying, "Let each man have his own wife and each woman her own husband."

In reality we trust Christ most fully not by sitting idly, but by taking careful, prudent action which we have reason to believe is in line with his will. While there is a certain trust implied by sitting passively and waiting for God to dump the love of your life into your lap, there can be a greater trust involved in taking the often scary steps of changing your circumstances or beginning a new relationship. Such steps are not incompatible with having faith in Christ. When bathed in prayer and a desire to honor him, they are a vital part of what walking in faith involves.

The Call to Accountability

This brings us to the third perspective which is vital in seeking marriage. Scripture takes the highest possible view of marriage, deeming it a relationship comparable to that of Christ and the church (Eph 5:21-33). To this end I must strive for the highest possible reverence for Christ at each point as I consider the possibility of marriage and take practical steps to bring it about. Thus Paul commands, "For this is the will of God . . . that each of you know how to take a wife for himself in holiness and honor" (1 Thess 4:3-4 RSV).

This statement speaks to the importance of taking my daily walk with Christ seriously—the need for faithfulness to personal devotions, Bible study, worship, fellowship and support groups. Growing in Christ not only will prepare me to be a better companion to my spouse but will enhance the Lord's freedom to work out his best in my life, for marriage and all areas. Part of this growth process is praying regularly about my hopes for marriage. I should give attention both to asking God for grace to do his will and to expressing honestly what my desires are at the present time. Finally, this passage speaks to the need to make the most responsible, sanctified decisions I can as I take steps to find a relationship and, ultimately, as I decide about whether to marry a particular person. At each point my goal should be to understand and do God's will.

While knowing that God wants me to seek a relationship with him presents a challenge, it brings me back to a basis for hope as well, for it reminds me that he wants to work for good at all points in my life. He is not my adversary but my friend, one who desires the very best for my future. As the psalmist declares: "He redeems my life from the pit and crowns me with love and compassion. He satisfies my desires with good things, so that my youth is renewed like the eagle's" (Ps 103:4-5). That is incentive enough to seek to honor Christ in every way as I take steps toward marriage!

Four

....

How Can I Know
God's Will?

I MUST ADMIT THAT I DECIDED TO ASK EVIE TO MARRY ME WITHOUT receiving any direct revelation to do it. I deeply wanted God's will and, in fact, made my choice during a day set aside for prayer and meditation. But I approached the decision more rationally than mystically. I weighed the pros and cons. In the end I decided to propose to her mainly because it seemed to make the most sense to do so.

If this sounds like a bit of true confessions, it's not because I'm doubting now that I made the right choice. Far from it! Yet I now realize that as a young believer I wasn't always at home with such a practical approach to decision making. There were many people telling me how to know God's will during that time, most of them saying that I should wait for God to show me in a dramatic and clear-cut way what to do.

Gradually, as I became more acquainted with Scripture, I began to see it presenting a rather different—and, frankly, more liberating—picture of guidance. While the early people of faith were strongly confident that God was leading them, in only a few instances in the Bible do we see them receiving dramatic guidance from God. They tended to make their decisions in a logical manner, even taking major steps of faith without any supernatural leading. By the time I decided to marry Evie, I had grown fairly comfortable with taking a practical approach to major decisions. Still I went back and forth on the question of how to seek God's will.

Since that time I've studied Scripture intently on the matter, and my first book was devoted to the topic of guidance. I can now say confidently that this *is* the approach to guidance that is recommended in the Bible. God is pictured as one who guides through our rational decision process, not apart from it. There is abundant evidence that guidance, as one writer has put it, usually boils down to sanctified thinking.

I find that Christian singles today, though, are more typically at the point where I was as a young believer—not fully comfortable with this idea. Many feel guilty even thinking of the marriage decision as a "choice."

"Shouldn't you wait for God to impress his will on you in some unmistakable manner?" they ask. "Isn't it wrong to make much effort to think things through?"

Voices preaching such notions about God's will continue to prevail throughout our Christian culture. Three especially common perspectives on guidance discourage practical thinking and often cause confusion for those considering marriage.

With the Heart or with the Mind?

One teaching is that a decision for marriage should be approached intuitively rather than rationally—more with the heart than with the mind. While this is not a uniquely Christian concept, it is often adopted in a particularly Christian way to explain how we receive God's guidance.

I first heard this belief proclaimed by a pastor whom I greatly respected, in a talk which he gave on the first retreat I attended as a new Christian. He said, "When you've met the person God wants you to marry, you'll know instinctively that this is the one. You won't be able to explain your choice. Yet you'll have no doubt at all that it's God's will. If anyone asks you how you know, all you can say is 'I know in my heart that this is the right person.' If you can give a reason for your choice, then it's not God's leading."

I remember with amusement how later in the same retreat another pastor from the same church, whom I also highly esteemed, addressed the same issue in a talk. Not having heard the first pastor's talk, he declared, "It is vital to use your mind in selecting a marriage partner. You need to have good reasons for your choice. Beware of making this decision without carefully thinking it through." To say the least, as a new Christian I was thoroughly confused!

I must say in deference to both of these men that they both have had excellent marriages. I have no question that they each made a good choice, one through an intuitive approach, one through a more rational one. It suggests that God creates some of us to be more intuitive by nature and some more cognitive.

Yet I've also known many Christians who entered marriage with great conviction of heart, knowing for certain that God was leading them, but whose marriages have not endured nearly as well. About half of the ones I'm thinking of have ended in divorce. In many cases it now seems only too plain that the decision to marry was based too much on an inner impression and that not enough time was taken to assess whether the broad sort of compatibility needed for a marriage commitment was really there.

I've known so many, too, who thought that they had an inner leading to marry someone who never came to share their conviction. If I confess others' sins here, I must confess my own also. One afternoon as a young Christian I was praying in a pleasant mountain park setting when my thoughts wandered to a certain young woman in the college fellowship, a woman whom I knew only casually. As one thought led to another, I mused over what it would feel like to be married to her. The feeling was good. I concluded that God was giving me a vision that we would someday marry.

I had the audacity (though of course I didn't think of it that

way at the time) to go and share my "vision" with this woman—
only to be told that God had not spoken to her in any such way.
In fact, she made it clear that she had no interest whatever in a
romantic relationship with me.

Yet for some time after that I continued to cherish the conviction that she would someday come to her senses and see God's
will as I did. Neither friends nor pastors could convince me of
the folly of my thoughts. I knew that God had spoken to me, and
that was that.

I could fill this book with stories of Christians who've shared
similar experiences with me. Many men and not a few women
have told me of receiving a vision to marry someone—a leading
that was never experienced by the other. And I've counseled
with so many, especially women, who have been at their wits'
end in knowing how to deal with a presumptuous friend who is
laying such a mandate on them.

I've seen time and again the unfortunate delusions that can
come from thinking that one's instinct is the unfailing voice of
God. Sadly, I've also been close to some relationships which would
have made excellent marriages, yet one or the other was waiting
for a degree of inner conviction that wasn't reasonable to expect.

Why then does the intuitive approach, which seems to work
so well for some, present so many problems for others? Here it's
important to understand what the experience of intuition actually is. When we experience a strong inner conviction, a sudden
flash of insight or sense of inner leading such as I had on the
mountain, the experience should be understood not primarily as
a spiritual but a *psychological* one. Our mistake comes in thinking
that intuition is the direct voice of the Holy Spirit and thus a call
to action which is permanently laid upon us. In reality intuition
is a glimpse into our subconscious mind. It tells us what we are
really thinking and feeling deep down underneath.[1]

Thus intuition is very important, for our subconscious mind often
does a much better job of processing information than our conscious
mind does. Yet in the end our intuition is only as good as the infor-

mation that has gone into it. A sudden flash that God wants me to marry a certain person is invariably influenced by all the ideas I've ever been exposed to about the ideal mate. Yet new information and new understanding may lead to a new sense of intuition.

From this standpoint, I always have the right to question my intuition. I'm never bound to follow its mandate, and I never have the right to try to lock someone else into its dictate. When in a serious relationship I've really taken the time to get to know the other person, and when we've explored the possibility of marriage in sensible ways, then I can begin to trust what my intuition tells me. Yet often the conviction that comes at this point is quite different from impressions I had at the beginning of the relationship. In one survey of over a thousand happily married people, 80 percent "reported they did not feel an immediate attraction to each other when they first met."[2]

This is not to suggest that my inner impression must be unwavering before I can go ahead with marriage. Many of us are so constituted psychologically that such unerring certainty simply isn't possible. This is a point I want to return to in a moment. Here let it simply be said that the marriage decision should be made as much with the head as with the heart. God has commanded that we love him with all our mind as well as with all our heart, and it's vital that we apply the mind he's given us to the most important choice—aside from choosing to follow Christ— that we are ever privileged to make.

Do I Need a Special Sign?

While some Christians place too much weight on intuition, others assume that they need a special sign from God about whom to marry. The problems that result from this assumption are similar to those that come from spiritualizing intuition.

Some couples who have good reason to consider marriage hold back in the belief that they need a special indication from God to go ahead. Rick and Sandy had dated for over two years. They told me that they had asked God to give them a sign by a certain date to continue their relationship. Otherwise they would break up. When I asked them what specific sign they expected, they said that they didn't know. They simply wanted God to show them in some unmistakable way what to do.

Rick and Sandy illustrate the irony that is common to many who look for a special sign from God—the fact that often there is no clear idea what precisely that sign should be. This ambiguity leaves many Ricks and Sandys waiting indefinitely for marching orders.

It leaves others open to seeing signs that are not really there. A couple in the first church I attended met initially on a vacation trip to Europe. Later they encountered each other unexpectedly in a church in the United States. They took this extraordinary coincidence as a sign from God that they should marry. Tragically, their marriage lasted only six months. They simply had not done their homework in getting to know each other and in thinking through whether they were compatible or ready to marry. They were too quick to read supernatural guidance into an unusual circumstance.

To be sure, some Christians do specify to God what sign they want, a practice often called "putting out a fleece," in reference to Gideon's experience in Judges 6. One notable Christian described how he sought God's will about whether to marry his girlfriend: He mailed letters to two different friends, praying that God would show his will by the timing of the replies, but not telling his friends what was on his mind. If replies came back on the same day, he would assume God wanted him to marry this woman; if they came on different days, this would mean God's answer was no. When return letters from both friends arrived in the same delivery, he concluded that God had spoken affirmatively, and he went ahead and proposed marriage.

I don't deny that God may on occasion honor such a fleece offered in innocence by a sincere Christian. Yet there is no biblical promise that God is bound to do so. In fact, we find no example in the New Testament after Pentecost of believers seeking God's will through a fleece; the last instance was the disciples casting lots for Judas's successor (Acts 1:21-26), which occurred before the Holy Spirit was given on Pentecost. This indicates, I believe, that the Spirit-filled believer has all the inner resources needed for wise decision making. "Fleecing" is generally a diversion from taking proper responsibility for our decisions.[3]

It's interesting that on those few exceptional occasions after Pentecost when extraordinary supernatural guidance was given, it was always to instruct the disciples to do something which they wouldn't have chosen on the basis of reason alone. Philip's guidance by the angel to leave the dramatic revival in Samaria and go off to a desert road is a good example (Acts 8:26-40). In the great majority of personal decisions noted in the New Testament, individuals determined God's will simply through logical thinking, apart from any unusual guidance. For what it's worth, apart from Joseph's revelation from the angel to marry Mary, there is no instance in the New Testament of anyone basing a marriage decision on supernatural guidance. Nor do we find any statement suggesting that one should seek a special sign in a marriage decision.

My advice to couples who are looking for a sign from God about whether to marry is that God will give them a sign. It will be the evidence that they are compatible and ready for marriage which they discover in the normal process of building a relationship. They will find it not through some unusual or supernatural indication but through getting to know each other and using the gift of judgment which God has given them to make wise decisions. Scripture promises that we who follow Christ have the mind of Christ (1 Cor 2:16). This mind is not a passive one that waits for information to be dumped into it but a mind that *thinks*. It's no less than the capacity to make wise judgments.

The question often raised at this point is what the meaning of Proverbs 3:5 is. It commands us, "Trust in the LORD with all your heart, and do not rely on your own insight" (RSV). Doesn't this imply that we *lack* the ability to make good decisions? It must be remembered, though, that Proverbs gives us numerous other commands that enjoin us to exercise wisdom and make sound decisions. By telling us not to rely on our own

insight, this verse cautions us against trying to resolve our decisions without trusting in the guidance and provision of God. The
point isn't that we should not strive to make good decisions. To
the contrary, when we've put our trust in Christ and earnestly
sought his direction, we have basis for an uncanny trust that he
is guiding our decision process.

Should Someone Else Make the Decision for Me?
While some Christians look for direct guidance through inner
impressions or special signs, others put great weight on the need
for someone else to tell them God's will. A popular seminar has
taught for years that parents, whether Christian or not, have
chain-of-command authority to decree God's will for the marriage choice of their children. While I don't find Christians as
quick to accept this premise anymore, some still hold it as gospel.

More common today is a philosophy of spiritual leadership which
holds that pastors or church elders have the authority to decide
whom those under their care should marry. A surprising number of
churches, including some large, dynamic ones, follow this ideology.
It is occasionally embraced by certain parachurch ministries as well.

Still other Christians believe that someone with a special gift
of prophecy may be able to tell you whom God wants you to
marry, even though that person may have no relation to you or
be in any special position of spiritual authority—or for that matter have had any previous acquaintance with you at all. Some of
the most tragic examples I've seen of one person claiming to
know God's will for whom someone else should marry have involved those claiming to have a gift of prophecy.

In one case a high school student who was far from ready for a
lifetime commitment married because a strong-minded adult in
his church prophesied that he should do so. In another case a
college freshman, Elizabeth, was told by an older woman in her
church that God wanted her to marry Ken, a man in the church
whom she scarcely knew. As an impressionable new Christian,
Elizabeth assumed that this older woman, who spoke with such

authority, had a handle on God's will. She opened herself to a friendship with Ken; in time a dating relationship developed, and Ken proposed marriage. By now Elizabeth was in love with him, and she accepted. Shortly afterward Ken broke the engagement and within one month married someone else.

When I met Elizabeth on a students' retreat, she was a college senior and had only recently overcome two years of severe depression over the incident. She felt not only the pain of rejection, difficult enough for most to endure, but also great confusion about the meaning of the prophecy. Was it Elizabeth's fault that it failed? Ken's? Or was the woman who prophesied misguided in the first place?

Experiences like this remind me how extremely important it is for each of us to have a clear understanding of biblical teaching on the role of others in personal guidance. Scripture does stress that counsel is crucial in our decision making. A number of times the Proverbs declare, "In a *multitude* of counselors there is strength." Thus wisdom comes from many counselors, not from the dogmatic view of a single individual. With a multitude of counselors will likely come a multitude of opinions. Through them, my mind is stretched to think more deeply and farsightedly about my decision. Even if what I end up doing differs from what anyone has advised me, I've still benefited greatly from the whole counseling process. I must take responsibility for my own decisions, calling the shots as best as I can. Never does Scripture teach that I must follow the dictate of any one individual.

But what about the claims of those who insist otherwise? The verse that is usually quoted to show that our parents' opinion must prevail in a marriage decision is Colossians 3:20: "Children, obey your parents in everything, for this pleases the Lord." Yet the Greek word for children *(tekna)* denotes a young child, not an adult son or daughter. The command simply does not, as is claimed, lay a mandate on grown children to continue to follow their parents' dictates. While the injunction to honor our parents is always with us, we're not held to a rigid chain-of-command obedience to their directives.

The same point applies to the authority of spiritual leaders. There's no indication that those in leadership positions in the New Testament had the prerogative to direct the personal decisions of those under them. Spiritual leaders were given great authority to direct the affairs of the church and to declare the doctrinal and moral will of God. But that authority didn't extend to the personal choices of parishioners, such as where to work or whom to marry.[4]

Neither does the New Testament teach that the gift of prophecy enables one person to know God's will for the personal decisions of someone else. Charismatic writer Michael Harper, who writes with great esteem for the gift of prophecy, notes that "guidance" is not one of its functions:

> Prophecies which tell other people what they are to do—are to be regarded with great suspicion. "Guidance" is never indicated as one of the uses of prophecy. For instance, although Cornelius was told by an angel to send for Peter (Acts 10:5), Peter himself was told to go with them through an independent agency (Acts 10:20). There may be exceptions to this—but if so they are very rare. This gift is not intended to take the place of common sense or the wisdom which comes from God and which manifests itself through our natural faculties.[5]

I'm comfortable telling Christians that while they should graciously receive the counsel others give them, they should be thick-skinned (though not discourteous) with those who insist beyond a reasonable point that they know God's will for them. I'm not helping others by letting them think they can play Christ in my life. God has not created any person to be able to handle such a role. And I'm not helping myself by letting someone else make a decision for me which God wants me to take responsibility for resolving. Knowing God's will for my life is *my* responsibility. Others can help. But they cannot replace my personal need for thinking carefully and, finally, coming to my own decision.

Five

....

Can I Be Certain?

RECENTLY A TWENTY-FOUR-YEAR-OLD WOMAN, RITA, PHONED ME, anxious for my advice. She had been through two dating relationships in which her hopes were seriously disappointed. Finally she had taken a step to keep the pattern from repeating. She told the Lord that she wouldn't date another man unless her mom was confident that he was the one she should marry. She was bound and determined not to make a mistake about God's will again.

After Rita had made her resolution, Tom asked her out. Her mom felt that Tom would make an excellent husband for her, so Rita accepted, eagerly hoping she had finally found the Lord's choice. The time with Tom was enjoyable and only intensified her hope. Yet six months had now passed, and she hadn't heard from him again.

Rita felt not only rejected but terribly confused about what all of this meant concerning God's will. How could her mother have been so confident and Tom not be following through? Should she simply assume that Tom was God's choice and continue to wait?

I told Rita that I admired her respect for her mother's opinion. Our parents' counsel is so important in our big decisions. Yet to expect her mom to know the mind of God unerringly in this matter was to lay a burden on her too great for any human to bear. Rita would ultimately need to make her own decision, weighing her mom's advice along with other factors.

Rita didn't dispute what I said, but in frustration she replied, "Then how can I know *for certain?*" If her mom's advice was not an infallible sign of God's will, what would be?

Here we came to the heart of her dilemma. Rita assumed that she could have certainty about God's will for her marriage choice apart from discovering it in the step-by-step process of building a relationship. Rather than seeing God's will as something to be discerned through her experience, she assumed it could be found in some external way beforehand.

Rita's assumption brings us to the heart of the problem behind the desire of most people for direct guidance. Underlying the desire for guidance through inner impressions, special signs or someone else's pronouncement is usually the belief that perfect certainty about God's will is attainable. While many would not go as far as Rita in thinking they must have certainty before *beginning* a relationship, many—probably most—Christians assume they need absolute certainty before deciding to marry someone.

An Understandable Desire

The desire for perfect certainty is only too easy to understand. We don't like making even minor commitments without the assurance that we've looked at all possible options and chosen the best one. Yet we may decide to join a church, declare a college major, take a job, even buy a home in less than full confidence that our choice is the best possible one. Granted, our commitment at these levels doesn't lock us in forever. Changes can always be made, and at least we'll have learned from our experiences. The marriage decision offers no such freedom. For Christians, who take the inviolability of marriage vows with steely seriousness, marriage is a no-turning-back proposition. As a twenty-seven-year-old friend of mine, whose decision to marry his girlfriend has been on-again, off-again, expressed it, "I expect to be married to her for fifty years. That's a long time to live with the wrong decision."

Our desire for perfect certainty in the marriage decision is also fueled by fantasies and idealized mental pictures of the romantic relationship. Since childhood we've seen it again and again in literature and the media: man meets woman and both instantly recognize that they've found their one true love. As a result, it's deeply ingrained in our minds that when two people are destined for one another, they know it with a certainty that's immediate and absolute.

Yet our Christian teaching does just as much to encourage such a notion. We've heard so many stories of those who knew that they knew that they knew, and we've heard it said so many times that when you've met God's choice you'll have no doubts at all. Our evangelical tradition, too, with its great and proper emphasis upon the sovereignty of God, leaves us assuming that a God who is all-powerful wouldn't possibly leave us with less than perfect certainty that we've found the one of his choice. To assume anything less would be irreverent, we say—an insult to the greatness of God and his ability to guide his children.

Faith and Feelings

Here, though, we must be clear about where certainty is promised by Scripture and where it isn't. Scripture declares that we who are born again of Christ have basis for immense confidence in him. We can be certain of his intention to grant us eternal life, as well as of his determination to guide us in the very best paths between now and when we go to be with him. John 10 attests that Christ takes the same sort of autocratic but benevolent authority in our lives that a good shepherd takes for his sheep. Through many beautiful, poetic statements John presents Christ as one who not only has our very best in mind but has the power and the determination to lead us into it.

When he has brought out all his own, he goes on ahead of them, and his sheep follow him because they know his voice. But they will never follow a stranger; in fact, they will run away from him because they do not recognize a stranger's voice. (vv. 4-5)

I am the gate; whoever enters through me will be saved. He will come in and go out, and find pasture. The thief comes only to steal and kill and destroy; I have come that they may have life, and have it to the full. (vv. 9-10)

My sheep listen to my voice; I know them, and they follow me. I give them eternal life, and they shall never perish; no one can snatch them out of my hand. (vv. 27-28)

The implication of the biblical promise of guidance is that when I desire God's will and am prayerfully seeking it, I may be confident that he is guiding my whole decision-making process. This means that the decisions I end up making are the ones he wants me to make. Clearly this promise extends to the most far-reaching decision most of us ever have to make as Christians: the decision about whether to marry.

Yet never does Scripture promise that we will necessarily *feel* certain, to the point of no hint of doubt, in the decisions we make. It's here that we must remember the timeless distinction between faith and feelings. Faith is "the conviction of things not seen" (Heb 11:1 RSV). In other words, it's the belief that something is true even though we have less than complete evidence to support our conviction. It's the decision to believe something even though some room for doubt remains. Where perfect certainty exists, there is no need for faith!

Substantial Certainty
This is not to say that faith is an unthinking or foolhardy attitude. We commit ourselves to trust in Christ's salvation, to yield our lives into his hands and to believe in the infallibility of Scripture, on the basis of substantial evidence that God exists, that he has revealed himself through Christ, that Christ rose from the

dead and that the Scriptures have been divinely inspired by him.
Yet we would be hard put to offer absolute proof for any of these
claims. We have chosen to make a leap of faith on the basis of
reasonable evidence, even *very* reasonable evidence, but not
proof. Proof would remove the need for faith.

It's in this same spirit that the decision for marriage is to be
made. We should allow generous time for getting to know the
other person, and we should give keen attention to all the compatibility factors that can make for a healthy union or a difficult
one. Yet for most of us the point comes where we must make a
leap of faith. We need to go ahead and commit ourselves in the
face of something less than uncompromising certainty.

Charlie Shedd, from his decades of experience in family counseling, addresses the issue of certainty in choosing a mate in *How
to Know If You're Really in Love—Really in Love Enough for Marriage.*
He relates a letter a young woman sent him and then his response:

> Dear Dr. Shedd: Terry and I have been going together for over a
> year now and he keeps asking me to marry him. He really is great
> in so many ways, and I don't know what's the matter, but somehow
> I can't make up my mind. Is there any way a girl can be one hun-
> dred percent sure so that she never ever doubts? Please can you
> help me decide?

[Response:]

> Wish I could, but should anyone ever try to be one hundred per-
> cent sure? I doubt it. Those who say they are absolutely certain,
> with never a look back, may have turned their brains off. They
> could be living on emotion, minus intellect. So the goal is to begin
> at fifty-one percent surety, then build that to seventy-five, eighty-
> five, ninety.[1]

I like the way Dr. Shedd puts it. As we move ahead, our sense
of certainty can increase. Yet for most of us, the 90 percent level
is probably about it. Most of us are so constituted that perfect

certainty about anything is simply not a realistic goal. Those of us who are deep thinkers too quickly see possible exceptions to our conclusions. In the marriage decision we realize that we've met only a minute number of the opposite sex, and our acquaintance time with the one we're considering marrying has been extremely brief compared to the span of time we expect to be married. It's simply not reasonable to think that we could muster such a heroic degree of certainty that all measure of doubt is gone.

Deciding to Decide

Those of us who by nature are more feeling-oriented may indeed feel strongly assured at a given time that we have found the one for whom we were destined. Yet given new discoveries about our loved one or about ourselves, given new circumstances, given indigestion or a poor night's sleep, our feelings may change. If we simply look at how convictions in other matters have wavered in the past, we must conclude that we can't bank on the intensity of our present conviction continuing forever.

Yet we can take control of our lives. We can conclude that in spite of lingering uncertainties or mood swings, we do have substantial evidence that we and another would make good life partners and that we are both at a point of maturity where it makes sense to go ahead with marriage. This is the very good news part of what we're saying—it's okay to go ahead with even a commitment as momentous as marriage with less than perfect certainty. Indeed, it's not only okay but *necessary* for most of us if we want to do the kind of inertia-breaking needed to forge a marriage commitment.

I realize that some will claim the perspective I'm recommending is something less than the victorious life in the Spirit that the New Testament proclaims. I would contend just the opposite. It's when we have the opportunity to go ahead with a decision in the face of substantial but less than perfect certainty that the greatest opportunities for walking in faith occur. By choosing to marry someone on this basis, I'm thrusting myself into the hands of Christ, trusting that he is too big to let me make a mistake—or that if I have, he'll find a way to redirect me.

It's among those who are banking on perfect certainty that we often observe the least victorious spirit. Many who are in solid relationships which would make excellent marriages are waiting endlessly for a level of certainty that is simply not reasonable to expect. Others, like Rita, are locked into unhealthy situations because they believe God has given them a sign that they must stay there.

Some of the most tragic situations I've seen involve those with highly sanguine personalities, who are subject to strong mood swings, who go back and forth in their conviction to marry. One such woman whom I've counseled with has called her engagement on and off about a half-dozen times. Though she is a deeply intelligent woman in her young thirties, holding a challenging job in the medical profession, she's letting an unreasonable ideal of certainty control her decision about marriage, rather than her own good judgment.

Confronting Your Ambivalence

Those of us who find ourselves over a long period of time going through extreme emotional swings that make commitment difficult may profit from professional help. Underlying these mood swings may be a fear of commitment itself. With a skilled counselor we can explore factors in our background that contribute to this fear. We may likely discover that our childhood experience of love was inconsistent, leaving us gun-shy about trusting ourselves to anyone who professes too strongly to love us now. While such discoveries are painful, it is far easier in the long run to deal with reality than with emotional surges which we don't understand. With the right help we can come to terms with our past in a way that puts us in a better position to make confident choices in the present.

Yet we may also have to come to terms with our view of God's guidance. If we're cherishing the assumption that we can achieve perfect certainty before undertaking major steps, we need to revise that belief. The Christian life is not a fantasy experience where our life moves are constantly revealed in neon lights or through unswerving mystical impressions, leaving us with no need to think or wrestle things through.

To the contrary, Scripture portrays the Christian experience as an adventure of faith, where we never know what is around the bend—we inch ahead a step at a time. We always have just enough light to take the next step, yet we need to take that step in order to see clearly enough to take the step beyond. While we have great confidence in the one who guides us and protects us, we are constantly in the position from the human standpoint where we must take steps that seem to be risks. Yet it is precisely such steps that incline us most fully to trust in Christ, who alone knows the future and who alone can continue to give us the light unto our path. Through the whole experience comes a sense of life that, while often challenging, is never boring.

The marriage decision is in no way exempt from this adventure of faith. Indeed, it is often the greatest opportunity life offers to experience what walking in faith involves.

Part Three

Choosing a Spouse

Six

....

Do You Feel
Deep Compassion
for the Other Person?

"YOU'RE A WONDERFUL WOMAN, JAMIE. IN FACT, REMARKABLE. Whoever marries you will be extremely fortunate. But I'm not that man. I just don't believe it's right for us to marry."

Harold rehearsed his lines over and over, steeling himself for the dreaded announcement he felt he must make. He would rather let his relationship with Jamie linger on indefinitely. Yet he knew that it wasn't fair to keep her tied up in a romance that might go nowhere. He owed her a clear answer so that she could get on with her life.

Harold (twenty-five) and Jamie (twenty-six) had talked long and often about marriage during more than two years of dating. But while Jamie had been convinced about marriage for some time, Harold remained confused, not certain that his affection for her had the intensity of marriage love.

Harold knew that he cared deeply for Jamie, and their friendship had been a source of great strength and encouragement to him. He had been, in fact, no less than astonished by their broad compatibility and many areas of common interest. Though physical attraction had been minimal on his part at first, it had developed in time and seemed to be growing.

Yet Harold knew he was capable of stronger physical and romantic feelings than Jamie aroused in him. Several women had done more to turn his head in the past. In several other ways, too, Jamie fell short of his ideals. She was less athletic and generally less ambitious than Harold assumed his wife should be. So Harold had concluded that the evidence that they should marry just wasn't strong enough. The only reasonable step was to level with Jamie and break things off.

As he came close to telling Jamie, though, he was filled with remorse at the thought of disappointing her. He realized how much he wanted to make her happy. The thought of bringing her joy through marriage brought him immense pleasure as he mused on it. It was almost startling to face.

He was struck, too, with how much he wanted her to succeed. It was exciting to imagine her finishing her master's degree and finding the research position she had long dreamed of. He enjoyed thinking about how their supportive relationship could enhance her success.

Wisely, before making a final decision, Harold decided to seek counsel from an insightful pastor friend who knew both him and Jamie well. After sharing for nearly an hour about the relationship and his confusion over marriage, Harold concluded by saying: "Pastor Bill, I really want what is best for Jamie. I long for her to be happy. Yet I think it would be wrong to marry mainly from sympathy."

Pastor Bill quickly replied, "I agree with you, Harold. Marriages based on sympathy are bound for disaster. Yet the feelings for Jamie that you described to me are not sympathy but compassion. Marriages based on compassion are bound to prosper."

"What is the difference?" Harold asked.

"Sympathy is merely feeling sorry for someone," Pastor Bill replied. "Compassion is more positive and dynamic. You desire the other to be happy, to prosper, to experience God's very best."

Then after a long pause, Pastor Bill said gently but firmly: "I've got news for you, Harold. You're in love with this woman. You'd be crazy to let this one get away."

Identifying the Feeling

It may seem strange to suggest that someone would have to be told that he or she is in love. This flies in the face of the popular notion that when true love strikes, the sensation is so overwhelming that you have about as much chance of missing it as you would a rhinoceros in a wading pool. Yet cases like Harold's are common. There's a subtle nature to marriage-quality love which can easily escape our notice. This is especially true when we've been programmed, as Harold was, with ideas that hit wide of the mark of what marriage love is all about.

Many, like Harold, have so set their expectations that they are slow to identify healthy love when they actually experience it. Others fall into the pattern of thinking that passionate attraction will provide the basis for a sound marriage.

What then is the essence of marriage-quality love? Pastor Bill was right. Compassion is the basis of it. While the marriage bond requires more than compassion—friendship and sexual attraction are important—compassion is the heart of it.

There are many feelings which can attract and bond you to someone else. When love is truly from God, foremost among these is compassion. You feel the other's hurts and concerns as your own. You ache to see God's best worked out in that person's life.

The dazed sensation which we call "being in love" often has little to do with compassion. It can come from sexual attraction alone or from being enamored with qualities you esteem in the other. It can come when the other makes up for a deficit in your own life. It can come from the wonderful gratification of knowing that someone else cherishes you exactly as you are.

Pastor Jim Conway says it simply: Someone "may say, 'I'm in love with you,' but what he really means is, 'You meet my needs and make me happy.'"[1]

Don't get me wrong. When God gives you marriage-quality love for another person, you'll have great hope that the other will meet your needs. This is an important part of the emotional mix that melds you to another person's life. Paul says clearly in

1 Corinthians 7 that unless you need the benefits of marital companionship, you should stay single.

Yet when love has been brewed in your heart by God, you're possessed with a deep and often surprising desire to meet the other person's needs as well. Early on in my relationship with Evie I began to realize that I felt compassion for her more strongly than I had in other dating relationships. This was a crucial factor in concluding that God was prompting us to get married. And compassion has been an important motivating factor in our twenty-seven years of happy marriage. Such selfless love does not come easily to me and can only be supernatural.

Assessing Your Compassion

If you are in a serious relationship and considering marriage, let me suggest a test. Imagine something unfortunate happening to the person you're thinking of marrying. Picture him or her being rejected or fired from a cherished job opportunity, failing a program in school or having some experience which would be a blow to his or her self-esteem. Does the thought of this happening fill you with sorrow? Or does it bring you a certain gratification and relief?

When your affection for another person is based mainly on what they can do for you, you may actually rejoice inwardly at their setbacks (though feigning sorrow on the outside), for you perceive that their misfortune will make them more dependent upon you. At the same time you feel intimidated by their accomplishments. And you may feel terribly uneasy if they have strong friendships outside of your relationship.

When compassion is strong, you find yourself naturally desiring what is best for the other person. You're not threatened by the thought of their success—indeed, you rejoice in it. The requirements of 1 Corinthians 13 and Ephesians 5:21-33 don't seem like duties but as guidelines that are natural to fulfill. Not that there aren't times when you feel jealous or fearful of losing the other's affection. None of us is perfect, and humanness invades every relationship. But overall, you are comfortable with the other person developing their gifts, having successful experiences and even special friendships outside of your own. And when the other suffers a disappointment, you feel it with them.

Compassion in Scripture

Though Scripture gives few examples of couples in the courtship or engagement stages, there are two which provide striking pictures of compassion. We see a magnificent demonstration of compassion in the way Joseph, the father of Jesus, treated Mary. Though we're told little about this intriguing man, what we are told shows that he had an exemplary love for his wife-to-be.

When Joseph discovered that Mary was pregnant, it is said that he resolved to break off the relationship quietly (Mt 1:19). At this point Joseph didn't know that Mary's pregnancy was of supernatural origin but assumed she had been promiscuous. What's amazing is that Joseph didn't make a public display of Mary's unfaithfulness. He had every right to do so—in fact, he would have been expected to do so in order to save face for himself. But he resolved to break the engagement in the way that would be least humiliating to her. He showed great compassion for her even in the midst of this apparent transgression.

I have little question that Joseph's gracious spirit was an important reason God trusted him with the gift of marriage to Mary and the privilege of being the human father of our Lord.

Another impressive example of compassion is Boaz's treatment of Ruth in the book of Ruth (Ruth 3—4). Boaz awakes at midnight to find Ruth sitting at the end of his bed. Though he could easily have taken advantage of her in this vulnerable and enticing situation, he resisted all inclination to do so. And though his subsequent decision to marry her suggests that he greatly wanted her for his wife, he first allowed a closer kin the opportunity to exercise his right to marry her. He showed kindness and fairness at every point.

It is of considerable interest to me that both Joseph and Boaz were willing to accept even the ending of a relationship, as painful as that option might be. This is always the response of compassionate persons, when they know it's in the best interest of the other. It's in the unhealthy, addictive relationship that one feels that he or she must hold on to the other at any cost.

This is an important point, for sometimes one takes their own willingness to terminate a relationship as an indication that their love is not sufficiently strong for marriage. Ironically, the very willingness to let the relationship go may indicate that compassion is strong enough to warrant marriage. This was part of what convinced Pastor Bill about Harold's love for Jamie. It has also persuaded me on different occasions to encourage someone to take a second look at a relationship they were thinking of abandoning.

I don't, of course, mean to suggest that the willingness to end a relationship always suggests that true marriage-love is present. Many times it does not. Yet sometimes it shows in a paradoxical way that love runs deeper than one realizes.

Sorting It Through

If you find yourself, like Harold, confused about how to interpret your feelings for someone whom you're dating, and especially if it has been a long-term relationship, I would strongly recommend finding a qualified person with whom you can talk things through. A trusted Christian friend in an enduring, healthy marriage is a good bet. Or a pastor. I personally count it one of my greatest privileges to be able to help someone in this area. I know most pastors feel the same. You needn't be hesitant about approaching your pastor on this matter.

If you realize that you don't feel true compassion for the person you're thinking of marrying, this means two possible things. Either God is not calling you to marry this person, or else you need to allow more time for compassion to grow. In any case, it wouldn't be right to think of marriage to this person at this time.[2]

On the other hand, if compassion for your prospective partner is strong, realize that you have the single most important indication that your love is from God and is of the quality that can make for a healthy marriage. As undramatic as your feelings for this person may seem to be, you may be experiencing the seeds of a dynamic marriage-quality love. Even though you don't feel dazed, crazed or moonstruck over this person, if you truly *care* for him or her, you have the most essential ingredient for a vibrant marriage.

A Two-Way Street

I must add that it's just as important that the other feels compassion for you. It might seem that the most self-sacrificing, most Christian thing to do is to go ahead and marry someone for whom you feel deep compassion, even though it's not reciprocated. But as noble as the idea might sound, I can assure you that it is *not* God's will for you.

God's ideal for marriage is one in which two people share both compassion and personal fulfillment. Though we can argue that it should be otherwise, in reality your ability to give of yourself in marriage is at least partly dependent upon the fulfillment you receive from your spouse. This is how God has created us as humans, and we cannot escape the fact. There is give and take in every healthy marriage; if it's all give on your part and no receiving, eventually your steam will run out. You don't have what it takes to be a savior to someone in marriage, and God isn't calling you to take on that role.

Realize, too, that you'll not be helping the other person by allowing him or her to experience for a lifetime the benefits of your compassion without being expected to make a similar response. God's desire is that this person also grows into a compassionate, responsible individual. If your partner's response of compassion toward you is strikingly less than yours, he or she may stagnate at that point and not be challenged to grow into a more loving person. Don't expect that your influence—or marriage itself—will change your partner. The most compassionate thing you can do for this person is to not marry him or her.

If, however, compassion is strong on both sides of your relationship, rejoice! If it's matched with compatibility at other points which we'll look at, you have a sound basis to proceed with marriage.

Seven

· · · · · · · · · · ·

Are You Good Friends?

ONE OF THE MOST ESSENTIAL PRINCIPLES IN CONSIDERING MARRIAGE is so basic it can elude you. Is there a solid basis of friendship in your relationship? Do you enjoy being together and relating together in a creative variety of ways?

This isn't to say that friendship alone assures a good marriage. Friendship may be based on factors that don't build the two of you up and strengthen your relationship to Christ. You don't have to look beyond Scripture to find many examples of couples who led each other down the primrose path.

Yet when friendship is mixed with compassion and Christian maturity, you have a solid foundation for marriage. As with compassion, though, it's easy to overlook the significance of friendship in looking for more dramatic indications of romantic love. Friendship may seem too unspectacular a basis for marriage. Hollywood has programmed us to think of romantic love as something dramatically different from friendship—even the antithesis of friendship.

Consider the theme we see so frequently: A man and woman who are antagonists suddenly find themselves inexplicably attracted to each other. A fiery, passionate relationship ensues and they live happily ever after. Thus the expression "Love and hate are the same emotion with different names."

But while this theme makes for good entertainment and definitely appeals to our sense of adventure, it spells disaster for marriage. It's simply naive to think that romantic chemistry will triumph over all the problems of incompatibility in a relationship. In reality, the day-to-day demands of marriage are such that unless two people enjoy being together in many ways besides romantically, the relationship will not likely endure.

On the other hand, when friendship is strong, there is a solid foundation for romance to grow, even within the most stressful conditions of family life. I challenge you to look carefully at any marriage relationship which impresses you. Talk to the couple. You will undoubtedly find that at the basis of the relationship is a strong and enduring friendship which could well survive apart from the marriage. In *Till Death Do Us Part,* researchers Robert and Jeanette Lauer aptly note, "Successful couples regard their spouses as friends, the kind of person they would want to have as a friend even if they weren't married to them."[1]

I'm aware of many excellent marriages, also, which began as good friendships with no romantic expectations. In some cases it took quite a while for interest in marriage to blossom. The point is crucial to keep in mind, for we're programmed to think that marriage-love more typically occurs at first sight. That belief can hinder you from giving a friendship a fair chance to develop into something more. Many, in search of some romantic ideal, never realize the potential that exists in a friendship they already have.

Of course, the positive side is that the seeds for a good marriage may be present in a friendship you now have, even though neither of you has thought about it. Again, remember the survey we noted in chapter three: one thousand happily married people were interviewed. A full 80 percent admitted they had not at first been attracted romantically to the one who became their spouse. It suggests that love at first sight—especially genuine, dynamic marriage-love—is the definite exception, not the rule.

With each passing year I come more and more to appreciate

how rare genuine, lasting friendship actually is. As a young person, I took friendship very much for granted. Now I'm embarrassed to admit how many friendships which seemed so significant at the time have fallen by the wayside. I count those which have endured as pearls of great price. If you have a deep, trusting friendship with someone of the opposite sex, count it as an extraordinary gift. It may or may not be a basis for marriage. But don't be too quick to dismiss the possibility just because romantic chemistry isn't yet there.

Priscilla and Aquila

It's striking that most biblical pictures of married couples are negative. When you search the Scriptures for examples of married individuals who had a redemptive influence on one another, you find them few and far between. Remarkably, in the New Testament Priscilla and Aquila are the only couple shown in a positive light at any length after Pentecost. What is most apparent from the passages that mention them is that more than anything else they were good friends.

Their friendship stretched to numerous areas. For one thing, they were in business together, as tentmakers (Acts 18:3). I doubt there is any greater test of friendship than the ability to work together in a common trade. The sheer amount of time spent together quickly takes the edge of novelty off any relationship. The potential for ego conflicts, annoyance over each other's idiosyncrasies, disagreement over finances and plain boredom is enormous. Yet the quality of their friendship even in this challenging environment was such that Paul himself was drawn into camaraderie with them and became a fellow partner in their work. In time their congeniality opened them to friendships with personalities as diverse as Apollos (Acts 18:24-28) and Timothy (2 Tim 4:19).

We also know that they traveled extensively and established homes in several regions. In the mere six passages which mention them, they are referred to in several different locales, including Rome, Corinth, Syria and Ephesus (Acts 18:1-3, 18, 24-28; Rom 16:3-5). When Paul wished to leave Corinth for Syria, they picked up and went with him. Considering the extreme travel conditions of the day, they had a most impressive sense of adventure. They enjoyed tackling challenges together, the bigger the better.

Of special interest is the fact that they formed churches in their homes. They shared not only business but pastoral responsibilities as well. They also studied together, grew intellectually together and exercised such a significant counseling ministry together that Apollos, a Billy Graham figure of the first century, was greatly influenced by their constructive criticism (Acts 18:24-28).

What I find most interesting is the fact that Priscilla's name is mentioned first in four of the six references to them (Acts 18:18, 26; Rom 16:3-4; 2 Tim 4:19). This suggests that she was more publicly visible and probably regarded as the more gifted of the two. This also tells us that Aquila was not intimidated by Priscilla's using her gifts and having a certain limelight of her own. He probably even encouraged her to cultivate and use her gifts. He must have been an unbelievably supportive husband, particularly considering the demeaning views held toward women in the first century. Perhaps more than anything this signifies the depth of their friendship and the level of compassion which Aquila felt toward his marriage partner.

The New Testament says nothing of romantic love between Priscilla and Aquila, though we can guess it was probably there. But whether or not they loved each other romantically, one thing is clear: they *liked* each other. I don't think we can overemphasize the importance of the fact that the Holy Spirit, in recording but one positive example of a married couple in the New Testament church, gave such attention to factors in their friendship.

Assessing Your Friendship

But what does this mean for your own relationship? On one

level judging friendship is easy enough. You instinctively know when the bond of friendship exists with someone and don't need anyone's formula for figuring that out. Yet determining whether your friendship has the qualities which would make for a good marriage can be more challenging. Let me suggest some guidelines for weighing this:

1. Do you have a variety of common interests? A friendship can develop because of a common involvement in one area. You might be drawn to someone in a drama club, for instance, because of your mutual love for acting. But if that attraction dries up or becomes impractical to pursue, will there be enough other areas to keep your relationship strong and on the growing edge? I don't mean that you must share all interests in common. It will be important for each of you to have individual pursuits as well. Yet you shouldn't consider marriage unless you have several significant points of common interest.

2. How well do you support each other at your points of strength? Do you find it natural to encourage the other to develop and use his or her gifts, even if they are not ones that you personally have? Does he or she find it natural to encourage you in this way? The way I've phrased the question is not accidental. I did not ask, "Are you willing to do this?" but "Do you find it *natural* to do so?" One of the most beautiful aspects of friendship is the way in which two people inspire each other to be the best they can be, helping the other always to appear in the best possible light. This is a vital dynamic for a marriage relationship.

3. How comfortable are you accepting the other's humanness and weaknesses? If you're thinking, "My partner doesn't have any significant problems or idiosyncrasies which I find annoying," you clearly don't know that person well enough to get married! In close friendship two people become acquainted well enough to find that neither is a plaster-of-Paris saint—each has qualities which are less than admirable. Yet friends find it natural to forgive and overlook many offenses. A missed phone call, a late arrival, a thoughtless remark, while irritating at the time, doesn't become a source of long-term contention. Friends instinctively realize that the good outweighs the bad in a relationship and that it's not worth accentuating the negative to the point that the positive is overshadowed.

Though you've undoubtedly heard it said many times, marriage is not likely to change things which you don't like about your partner. If the other has a characteristic you'd find unbearable to live with, then you should definitely not consider marriage. On the other hand, if you're comfortable accepting the other at the point of his or her roughest edges, even finding them laughable at times, then you have one of the most cherished qualities of friendship.

4. How often do you laugh together? Is there a lighthearted side to your relationship? Are you able to take good-natured teasing from each other, and others as well?

Just this week, a woman who has been through a marriage breakup told me that one of the most difficult parts of the relationship was the fact that her husband lacked a sense of humor. He couldn't laugh at himself.

In his insightful book *Love Is Not Enough,* Sol Gordon advises, "If it is extremely difficult for you to develop a sense of humor, please do not plan on raising a family; laughter is a compulsory ingredient when it comes to having children."[2] I would go practically as far in speaking of the relationship between husband and wife itself. While a sense of humor may not be the most essential aspect of a healthy marriage, it's far from the least significant. With Dr. Gordon I would rate it as more important even than sexual attraction.[3]

5. Do you build each other up in Christ? Again, friendships come in healthy and unhealthy varieties, as Scripture constantly shows. Overall, do you build each other up in Christ and encourage each other's spiritual growth? (We will look at this issue in greater detail in chapter eleven.) Are you likely to enjoy carrying out marriage responsibilities together? Picture yourself doing the things you will have to do together in family life—raising children, maintaining a home, carrying out the endless assortment of domestic chores. Do these tasks seem like activities that would be enjoyable to do together or routines that must be tolerated to enjoy the physical side of the relationship? Be honest. Over the years about 95 percent of your time together will be spent in domestic responsibilities, not in romantic intimacy. While of necessity these cannot always be scintillating tasks, you should at least have a general desire to share this area of life together.

6. *What about the physical side of friendship?* You can, of course, have a deep and lasting friendship with someone of the opposite sex in which no physical attraction is present. But in a relationship that has prospects for marriage, you will naturally be concerned about the potential for eros. Here several things should be kept in mind:

☐ Physical attraction can come at a later point, even when it isn't present at the beginning of a friendship. If other factors in your relationship are good, and at least the possibility of physical attraction is there, allow reasonable time for it to develop. Again, remember that most of us have to go through considerable deprogramming of unreasonable ideals in this area before we can enter into a physical relationship that is truly healthy.

☐ The physical relationship is not the panacea that it's often thought to be. In speaking of reasons to consider marriage, Sol Gordon notes aptly, "Frankly, sex alone is not worth it."[4] Remember that most of your time in marriage will be spent in other activities. If in all honesty the main focus of your concern and energy in the relationship is on the physical, then other aspects of friendship are probably not strong enough to recommend marriage.

☐ The level of physical attraction which you feel for each other may not have to be as overwhelming as you think to provide the basis for a good marriage. (This point is so important I'll devote considerable attention to it in chapter nine).

7. *Beware of unreasonable ideals.* Be careful of holding the friend-

ship up to unrealistic expectations. Pastor and author Larry Richards speaks of a woman whom he knew who divorced her husband because their marriage was only "90 percent good." For her, nothing less than perfection was acceptable; she left a 90-percent relationship to search for one that was 100 percent perfect.[5] Her attitude was not only naive but tragically self-defeating. For most of us, some revision of our expectations will be needed at virtually every point if we are to find a fulfilling marriage relationship.

Be especially cautious in comparing your present relationship with others you've had. While some comparing of this sort is usually unavoidable (all valuative thinking involves comparisons), it's easy to reach misleading conclusions. It's quite possible that a past relationship was more electrifying or dynamic in some particular way than your present one. It's all too easy, too, to overglamorize past relationships (or imagined future ones) and to miss the potential in a present one. Treat this relationship as an entity in itself. If it measures up well with the guidelines I'm suggesting, and if compassion between you is strong, you may well have an excellent foundation for marriage.

Friendship is a remarkable gift of God and one of the greatest luxuries of life which he allows us to enjoy. In marriage it is not merely a luxury but essential to fulfillment and fruitfulness on every level. Keep it high on your list of considerations in weighing the possibility of marriage.

Indeed, much of the secret to a good marriage is to marry a friend.

Eight

....

Are You Both Ready for Marriage?

IN MY FIRST YEAR OF SEMINARY I FELL INTO THE HABIT OF ARRIVING a few minutes late for a particular class. The professor called me into his office one day and told me bluntly that he was annoyed with the practice. Since he suspected I was eager for marriage, he added, "If you ever want to be married, you had better learn to be more punctual—your wife will find it intolerable to live with someone who can't manage time."

I had honestly never thought of it this way before. I was still quite naive in my thinking about marriage and assumed that love and being Christian would cover any problems that arose. Now it is only too clear that the professor was right. Maturity and lifestyle factors make an enormous difference in the ability of two people to live effectively together in marriage. As you consider your compatibility with someone, it's just as important to look carefully at how ready both of you are for marriage.

Judging Your Readiness for Marriage

Here are some important factors you will do well to consider.

1. The question of values. Do you both accept the biblical teaching that marriage is forever? There are many in our society who look upon marriage as an experimental option ("if it doesn't work, I'll get out"), and it's hard not to be affected by this mentality. If there's even the slightest thought in either of your minds of approaching the marriage experimentally, don't go ahead.

How much personal worth do each of you have tied up in making the marriage work? It's vital that each of you has a strong ego need to be part of an enduring marriage. It should be a significant matter of personal pride to see the marriage succeed. If either of you is at all indifferent about this, if the thought of the marriage ever breaking up seems less than devastating to you, then your motivation for a lifetime commitment is less than it needs to be.

It's important to look at both *what* each other's values are and *why* you hold them. We may buy into certain values simply because we inherit them from parents, absorb them from our Christian culture, go along with them to be accepted by others, believe them because they are "right." God gives us standards to live by because he understands much better than we do what will contribute to our long-term well-being. But unless we are convinced on the deepest level that we really will be *happier* following God's standards than going our own way, they will have little holding power when the chips are down.

We've all seen people who carry their values on their sleeves—preaching to others about the need for faithfulness in marriage—who cave in themselves when a sufficient enticement comes along. When you scratch beneath the surface, you usually find that they were holding their values unreflectively without really understanding why they were necessary.

2. Family history. While we are not fated to inherit the life patterns of our parents, they do form a certain default mode in our experience. If both sets of parents have had good marriages, the prospects of your own marriage being successful are enhanced. If parents of either of you have divorced, separated or had a difficult marriage, there's a greater than normal chance of that pattern repeating if certain stress factors occur in your marriage. If either of you is the child of an unhappy marriage, you need to be sure that you understand the factors that led to your parents' problems. It's vital that you have the self-understanding and determination to avoid the same destructive pattern. Here counseling is often beneficial.

3. Track records. What sort of success have you each had in keeping commitments in other areas of life—jobs, dedication to projects, past friendships and relationships? Is the evidence really there that you have the maturity to keep a commitment as enduring as marriage?

4. The age question. While the question of age is somewhat subjective, the odds are greatly in your favor if both of you are at least into your twenties. One study showed that divorces in American families where both married under the age of twenty-one were six times the national average.[1] In the island community where I go to write, thirteen of a flock of fifteen high school marriages ended in divorce. If either of you is a teenager, I strongly recommend—though I know it's hard—that you wait until both of you are at least twenty-one before marrying.

5. How much experience has each of you had living independently? This is a more significant issue than the age question. It's normally unwise to marry before each has lived at a full responsibility level independent of parents for at least two years. "For this reason a man will leave his father and mother and be united to his wife, and they will become one flesh" (Gen 2:24). If you feel compelled to go on living with a parent, you're definitely not ready for marriage. I'm not speaking here of the special situation where you decide (as a mature, free choice) to care for an infirm parent or relative, and you and your partner both agree on doing this. Though this often creates a stressful situation for a young couple, it can be a workable one. However, if either of you feels bound to continue living with a parent for security reasons, or from fear of disappointing the parent, then you don't own your own life sufficiently to enter marriage.

Of course, leaving parents means more than physical separation. You can live five thousand miles from your folks and still be strongly under the control of their expectations. While Scripture enjoins us always to honor our parents, we are called as adults to freely manage our own lives so that we may submit them in freedom to Christ. If you find great difficulty saying no to a parent, or if you are easily swayed by their wishes even when they go against your better judgment, you don't yet own your life adequately to give of yourself in marriage. I heartily recommend getting Harold Halpern's excellent book *Cutting Loose: An Adult Guide for Coming to Terms with Parents.*[2] Read it thoroughly, carefully consider the points he raises, and where appropriate follow his suggestions for gaining healthy (but respectful) independence from your parents before thinking further about marriage.[3]

6. How well do you manage time? My professor was right—good handling of your time is vital to effective functioning in marriage. No one can be punctual all of the time; emergencies do occur, and none of us ever perfectly manages the time that we have. Yet if either of you is frequently late, cannot be depended upon to keep a commitment or has difficulty saying no to someone in order to keep a commitment already made to someone else, you have a serious problem with managing time. You'll have difficulty in holding down employment—and in being an effective helpmate to your partner in marriage.

Fortunately, poor time management is a treatable ailment (I'm a case in point). Through making the effort, each of us can achieve greater discipline and gain greater control of our use of time. A book or seminar on time management can help. But if time management is a significant problem for either of you, don't think about going forward with marriage at this time. Deal with this problem first. Then allow at least six months of consistent improvement to demonstrate to yourself and your partner that you've genuinely changed.

Don't be fooled into thinking that marriage will cure the problem of managing time. If anything, it will make matters worse. Contrary to popular fancies, marriage doesn't bestow on us a magical ability to rise above time. The day-to-day realities of marriage are lived out *within* time. Thus, proper management of time is essential to a healthy marriage.

7. How well do you manage money? My question here is not whether you agree on what your standard of living should be (an issue we'll look at in chapter thirteen) but how well you live within the means you actually have. None of us is perfect in our handling of money. Yet if either of you frequently outspends your income or has trouble paying bills or keeping financial commitments, then you're probably not ready for the increased financial burdens of marriage.

I make this point less dogmatically than the others, for the division of financial responsibility varies from marriage to marriage, and couples sometimes balance out each other's strong and weak points in this area. But it's vital that together you look at how you plan to manage money in your marriage and grade yourself on how well you are likely to do it. If your mark isn't high, then you should get help in learning how to manage finances before going ahead with marriage. A college course in home economics, a seminar on financial management or sessions with a financial consultant may help.

8. Are you emotionally ready to forsake the benefits of the single life? Many who marry in their college or high school years, and some who marry well into adulthood, discover that they are not nearly as ready to let go of the advantages of singleness as they thought. Though the prospect of marriage was alluring, once the newness wears off they find themselves restless and longing for the freedom of movement they enjoyed before becoming attached. More than a few marriages break up over this tension.

Personalities vary greatly, as does the timing of individual growth, and some are ready to make the transition from singleness to marriage at a much earlier age than others. It is important that you each know yourself well enough to judge whether you are truly ready to make the tradeoffs involved. Especially if you or your partner are in your early twenties or below, I strongly recommend exploring the question thoroughly with a qualified counselor. Make sure you are not pushing yourself beyond reasonable limits in making this leap.

9. Length of acquaintance. Again, individuals and relationships differ widely, and it is impossible to lay down a rigid formula for acquaintance time before marriage. Some couples are able to make a mature decision about marriage in a fairly short period of time while others need several years to work things through. Generally it is advisable to allow at least a year for getting acquainted before you move into marriage. I suggest this not only because it usually takes that much time to get to know someone well enough to forge a lifetime commitment, but also because we are all seasonal creatures to some extent. It is important to understand how seasonal differences may affect both your individual personality patterns and the dynamics of your relationship.

10. Have you had the chance to observe each other under difficult conditions? Much more important than the length of acquaintance is the quality of it. A friend who endured a difficult marriage breakup confessed to me, "Before marriage we always saw each other on our best time." Marriage brought with it unexpected revelations about each other. It's true that in dating you tend to see each other under optimum conditions that bear little resemblance to the stresses of marriage. It can be hard to gauge what personality patterns will be like in the day-to-day realities of married life. (This is another reason why relationships that begin as friendships with no romantic pretenses often provide the best basis for marriage.)

Before entering marriage, it's important to have reasonable opportunities for observing how each other responds to stress, including major disappointments or failures and day-to-day annoyances such as getting stuck in traffic. Is the typical reaction a flash of anger, whining or withdrawal? Or is there the ability to rise above the situation and show congeniality and optimism even when frustrated? And how do you each respond when disappointed with the other? Do you tend to berate or belittle the other? Or does an atmosphere of forgiveness and constructive discussion more typically prevail?

I would strongly caution against marrying anyone who has poor emotional control. Here let me be especially clear in explaining what I mean. Anyone will lose their temper on occasion or react to disappointment in a less than commendable way. The mature person will later apologize, show remorse and make some effort to avoid repeating the pattern. The immature person will tend to prolong the response, wallowing in anger or self-pity, and may not apologize or make any meaningful effort to improve. I don't mean there is no hope that this person can change and grow. But until that happens, he or she shouldn't be considered a candidate for marriage.

Run, do not walk, away from a relationship with anyone who is in any way physically abusive to you—slapping, kicking, punching, pushing. (It's more common in Christian relationships than you think.) Under no condition—short of very clear and sustained evidence of reform through counseling—should you consider marrying such a person.

11. Are both of you free of chemical addictions? Under no circumstances should you consider marrying someone who has an active addiction to drugs or alcohol. You will buy into a lifetime of hell if you do. Don't bank on promises of reform or pledges to seek treatment. Even when they make promises with the very best intentions, addicts more often renege than carry through. If the addict does seek help or renounces the habit, you should allow at least a full year of freedom from the addictive behavior to pass, with no relapses, as evidence that genuine recovery has occurred before considering marriage to this person.

12. Is either of you desperate to get married? Do you feel that life will have no purpose if you can't get married? Are you expecting marriage to solve major personal problems? If so, then the marriage is headed for trouble before it starts. I don't mean that it's wrong to hope that marriage will improve your life; without that hope there's little sense in getting married. But I'm speaking of balance here. Unless you are reasonably content with the direction of your life apart from being married, you will lack the strength of character to be a supportive partner in marriage. As hard as it is to accept, you will do yourself and the other person a great favor by putting off marriage.

I would recommend, too, reading and studying at least one book dealing with the problem of addictive or unhealthy love. There are some excellent ones to choose from.[4] Give close thought to what really makes for healthy marriage-love, and take the steps needed to grow to the point where you can give and receive this kind of affection. In the end you'll be not only a happier person but also a much more effective marriage partner.

Toss Your Rose-Colored Glasses Aside

But how is it possible to get a realistic picture of each other in the rose-colored-glasses atmosphere of dating? It can take some effort. One way is to plan some activities together which will put you in more challenging social situations. Some suggestions:

☐ Go on a ski trip or backpacking expedition with singles from your church.

☐ Plan a weekend visit to parents or relatives who live out of town.

☐ Go on a short-term missions project together (a particularly good option from many angles).

☐ Commit yourself to weekly service together in an inner-city ministry or a nursing home.

Additionally, don't hesitate to talk with friends, family members or work associates of your partner and, where it can be done discreetly, ask them for an honest evaluation of that person's character and potential as a marriage partner. If this sounds conniving, remember that you are looking at spending the rest of your life with this person. If you were hiring someone for a business, you wouldn't hesitate to get references, even for someone employed for a short-term project. How much more important to be fully informed in preparation for the most binding commitment you'll ever make.

The Value of Counseling

As important as the issues raised in this chapter are, I realize that judging yourself or your partner at any of these points can be easier said than done. Some of us tend to be too lenient in such judgments, others too harsh. If there is any question how clearly you are seeing things, it is extremely important to get counsel from someone who is qualified to help with the marriage decision. Seek the best professional help available in your area, even if it means paying a fee for services. The amount you pay for sessions with a marriage counselor will probably be a drop in the bucket compared to the investment you've already made in education for your career.

I urge you, too, to go through a series of sessions in premarital counseling once you become engaged. Just recently a friend admitted to me, "My wife and I never had premarital counseling. We didn't take our first personality survey until we were four or five years into our marriage. Premarital counseling would have saved us a lot of headaches."

The pastor who marries you may offer such a service (and some insist upon it), but many do not. And while some take the process quite seriously, others mete out rather cursory advice in their sessions. Take advantage of the best help available to you, even if it means seeking out a professional who specializes in family counseling.

Marriage is too serious a step to do less.

Nine

··········

Are You Physically Compatible?

DON AND JEAN HAD DATED FOR THREE YEARS BUT HAD BROKEN UP several months before asking to talk with me. Both were mature, congenial Christians in their later twenties. Both held responsible jobs and were making good strides in their careers. In meeting with me separately, each stressed how much they cared for the other and how significant their friendship had been. Each had dreamed often of marrying the other, and at most points they seemed an ideal match. It was the issue of physical compatibility that was holding them back.

Don feared that his sexual attraction to Jean wasn't strong enough to justify marriage. "I simply don't feel the electricity in this relationship which I thought I'd experience when the right person came along—or that I know I'm capable of feeling," he explained. Jean also wondered if her physical attraction to Don was strong enough for marriage. Yet her greater concern was with Don's ambivalence toward her. She found it demeaning to think of marrying someone who was less than moonstruck over her.

At the same time each insisted that they were sexually attracted to each other, to the point that control had been difficult at times. The problem was not the absence of eros but that each fell short of the other's ideals.

Don and Jean are typical of many Christian couples I've known who have expressed similar confusion to me about the physical factor in relationships. The most common question asked by Christian men, in fact, is how intense sexual attraction must be to justify marriage. Many, like Don, fear that their physical attraction to someone whom they are otherwise quite compatible with isn't strong enough for marriage. Women sometimes raise the question too. More typically, though, their concern is like Jean's—whether to marry a boyfriend who has confessed that his sexual feelings are only moderate or that he still finds it possible to be attracted to other women. This seems to fall so short of the childhood dream of someone who'll cherish you as his only true love.

These concerns are only too understandable. The hope for sexual pleasure is a major motive for marriage, and the physical relationship itself is, for most of us, the highest symbol of unity and perfection in marriage. We fear any compromise that might jeopardize our happiness or suggest that the marriage is less than fully blessed by God. But while the physical relationship is important, many Christians place too much importance upon it. Some are looking for an intensity of attraction that isn't reasonable or healthy to expect. Others have unreasonable expectations about how their partner should feel about them.

After meeting only once with Don and once with Jean, I was persuaded that each was holding onto ideals that were neither realistic nor likely to contribute to their happiness in marriage, and I told them so. I was convinced, too, that they were a strongly compatible couple and that underneath they really did want to marry each other. While I was careful to stress that I wasn't giving them a divine oracle, I did tell them that I thought they'd do well to marry. I was overjoyed when a week later they announced their engagement. They've been married over four years now and are doing well.

Don and Jean bring me hope as I treat this topic, for I'm reminded that there are many who want to be shown where their ideals are unrealistic. They instinctively realize the importance of Christ's teaching that truth, and not fantasy, sets us free. It is hard to grow up in American society and not have your perspective on love and romance shaped more by myth than by reality. Yet there is a dearth of clear teaching on this subject in the body of Christ. So for those with ears to hear it, let me now say it emphatically: This is an area where our thinking tends to be formed much more by Hollywood ideas and popular Christianity than by Scripture and common sense. Certain myths about the physical relationship prevail, even within the body of Christ, and keep many from clear thinking about the marriage choice.

Myths About Physical Compatibility

Myth 1: Sexual attraction must be overwhelming before you decide to marry someone. Many assume that when they've met the one they are to marry, the sexual attraction between them will be strong enough to fuel the neon lights of Las Vegas. The notion of "romantic love" (whatever is meant by that) is usually at the heart of it. This belief leaves many like Don, who find themselves in a good relationship where eros is less intense than they thought it should be, confused. Others wait endlessly for that ecstatic relationship that never seems to come.

Scripture does teach that sexual attraction is important in marriage. As we have noted, in 1 Corinthians 7:1-7 Paul goes so far as to say that apart from a significant sexual need, one shouldn't marry. Paul's clear implication, too, is that two people considering marriage should desire to fulfill their sexual needs with each other. Interestingly, though, Paul never addresses the question of how strong sexual attraction must be to justify marriage.

Elsewhere Paul says, "For this is the will of God, your sanctification: that you abstain from immorality; that each one of you know how to take a wife for himself in holiness and honor, not in the passion of lust like heathen who do not know God" (1 Thess 4:3-5 RSV). Thus, sexual attraction can reach a level where it overrides good judgment and interferes with sensitivity in other areas of a relationship. When this counsel is considered along with the 1 Corinthians passage, it becomes clear that eros does not have to be volcanic to make for a good marriage.

Experience shows that the best marriages are often those where *moderate* physical attraction exists along with strong compassion, friendship and compatibility at other points. When eros is overwhelming, it can become obsessive and block growth and compatibility in other areas. The effect of extreme sexual attraction is not unlike that of a drug addiction. Your life revolves around the moment of physical encounter. The 95 percent of married life which must be spent apart from the physical relationship becomes dull and unstimulating. You find it hard to be compassionate and sensitive toward your partner when he or she isn't interested in making love.

Those who enter marriage with unreasonably high expectations for the sexual relationship are in the greatest danger of a letdown. If the couple hasn't nurtured other areas of interest, the marriage is headed for disaster before it starts. In the end it is the balance, or combination, of factors that makes for a happy and healthy marriage.

Myth 2: You will be more strongly attracted sexually to the person you are to marry than you've ever been toward anyone else. While this is true in some cases, it isn't in many others. Most of us are so constituted that we can experience sexual feelings—even very strong attraction—for virtually anyone of the opposite sex who fits certain stereotypes which we have been conditioned to find appealing. This includes many who would make anything but a good marriage partner for us.

It is possible that you have had a past relationship where eros ran stronger than it does in your present one. That is not a reason in itself to conclude that your present relationship is unfit for marriage. You may not have been as well matched at other points in the past relationship as you are now. Remember that it's always misleading to compare a single feature of relationships. Look at the combination of factors in your present relationship, and see what it suggests. Remember, too, that we tend to over-glamorize past relationships—to remember the happy moments and forget the difficult parts. Look at your present relationship as an entity in itself.

Myth 3: If either of you still finds it possible to be physically attracted to anyone else, then you aren't cut out for marriage to each other. I've known individuals who claim that they've never been physically attracted to anyone but their spouse. I find them, though, to be the rare exception (and possibly less than fully honest at that). Most of us do have the potential to feel sexual desire for more than one person, even at the same time. It is the nature of erotic desire that it can be invested in a variety of directions, a point that Paul seems to have well in mind in 1 Corinthians 7. When he advises Christians to marry "because there is so much immorality," his point is not "marry the one person who attracts you so strongly that you can't think of anyone else," but "because of the possibility of multiple attractions, determine to invest your sexual energies in one person—your spouse." This doesn't change the fact that I may be naturally inclined to be attracted to others, but it does underline the crucial need for commitment and determination not to let my interests stray outside of the marriage relationship.

Those in relationships like Don and Jean's often feel hurt and disillusioned when the other admits to having wandering fancies at times. Like Jean, they wonder whether God could want them to marry someone who even finds it possible to be attracted to someone else. My advice to those in Jean's situation, though, is to look more at your partner's ability and willingness to be committed to you than at the more intangible matter of whether his or her fantasies ever wander. In the long run it is the determination to stay loyal to you that will make the difference, not whether feelings ever run in other directions.

Be grateful, too, for your partner's honesty. Realize that most people in serious relationships have the same variety of feelings that your partner has confessed. Most simply are not as honest in admitting it.

The hardest part, of course, is dealing with your own self-esteem. In our hearts we each want to know that someone else loves us so greatly that the possibility of another affection never enters their mind. It's a blow to our pride to find that the reality of things is less than this ideal. But ultimately our security must be in Christ and not in another person, not even our spouse. Only when I can rest in knowing that Christ loves me as though I were the only person in existence, as Augustine put it, will I be able to fully enjoy a relationship with another human being whose capacity to love can never be perfect. It's through security in Christ that I can let go of childhood fantasies about romance and enjoy the reality of a marriage relationship for what it is.

Myth 4: Your physical attraction for the one you marry will never waver. This unfortunate notion simply ignores human nature. Both during courtship and during marriage itself there will be an ebb and flow to physical desire on the part of both of you. The important thing is not how you feel at a given hour or day but the pattern of attraction over time.

Myth 5: You will know instantly or early on in a relationship whether physical attraction can be experienced. This is perhaps the most misleading assumption of all, for it keeps many relationships with good potential from having the chance to develop. It's an unfortunate side of our love-at-first-sight myth. To an important extent physical attraction can be learned and developed, especially when compassion and friendship are already strong. While you shouldn't consider marriage if no eros is present, neither should you be too quick to conclude that it can never develop. Physical attraction that develops after friendship already exists is often more enduring than that which forms apart from friendship and so often becomes the main basis for a relationship. Unless friendship keeps pace, the physical flame eventually dies out.

Judging Physical Compatibility
But how can you actually know that you and another person will enjoy sex together in marriage? The answer is that you can trust

your instincts. Here it is perhaps necessary to refute yet another myth—the idea that you must experiment to find out if you are physically compatible with someone else. Throughout biblical times and for centuries thereafter (and still today, in some places), excellent marriages have been arranged by parents, who instinctively recognized that their sons or daughters would be physically compatible with someone else. In many cases, too, matchmakers filled the same function and were remarkably successful. If an outside party under the guidance of God can determine this for someone, without any direct evidence that the marriage will work, then certainly we who follow Christ can make this judgment for ourselves.

If you have gotten to know someone well, and you can imagine that you would enjoy sexual relations with this person in marriage, you can trust that insight as being as reliable as any discovery that would come from prolonged experimentation, if not more so. Rather than preach to you on the virtues of abstinence (which I could certainly do), let me simply encourage you to leave as much as possible in the physical arena to look forward to in marriage. This will add a greater dimension of joy to the early days of your life together.

I'm not denying that either of you may have inhibitions or attitudes which will interfere with a healthy sex life in marriage. Yet these can be discovered as well through discussion as through physical involvement before marriage. If these do exist, by all means get counseling and work them through before entering a lifetime of intimate relations.

Remember that God wills your success and happiness in marriage. As you look to him for wisdom, you can trust that he is giving you sound insight as you dream of the future and discuss this area together.

The Question of Frequency

The question remains whether it is necessary to have clear agreement before marriage on how frequently and when you will have sex. While I would strongly encourage you to talk about this, it's frankly impossible to predict what precisely your sexual needs will be at different points in marriage. Your sex drive will be affected considerably by a multitude of factors, including rest, health, age, weather, time of year, point in the menstrual cycle, children, work pressures, family stresses and, last but far from least, the state of your self-esteem.

It's extremely unlikely that both of you will always find your level of interest in the physical relationship to be at the same point. In a normal relationship there will be more times when one is eager and the other not than when both are equally inclined. Paul is straightforward in saying that when husband and wife are at different states of desire, preference should be given to the one with the sexual need (1 Cor 7:4-5). Again, we come back to the crucial elements of compassion, friendship and maturity in marriage, for each needs to be ready and willing to accommodate the other sexually even when desire is one-sided.

At the same time, compassion is a two-way street. Each should be willing to bridle his or her desire at times out of consideration for the other's state of interest. Over time you discover that sex is far and away most enjoyable when both strongly desire it. Quality is far more important than frequency. As you come to appreciate this, it becomes easier to exercise restraint and to plan love-making for the most favorable time.

What it boils down to is the need for a lot of give-and-take in the physical relationship—times when one accommodates the other, times when one restrains out of respect for the other's feelings, times when you agree together to set aside a special time for being intimate. As you think of the future, it's not so important to agree now on a schedule for intimacy as to determine whether the openness to this give-and-take is really there. Again, it comes down to compassion—the determination to will the other's best. This is the most essential ingredient for lasting physical compatibility in marriage.

What If Eros Is Overwhelming?

I've been discussing relationships in which individuals are uncertain about whether physical attraction is strong enough for marriage. I realize, however, that some readers have quite the opposite concern! You may be in a relationship where physical attraction runs very strong and wonder whether it's okay to marry with the velocity of eros this high. Or you may wonder how any other alternative besides marriage could possibly be considered given the intensity of your feelings.

Some Christians assume that they are virtually obligated to get married in this situation, given Paul's admonition (1 Cor 7) to seek marriage as a refuge against the temptation of having sex out of wedlock. Keep in mind, however, that Paul also warns against letting the physical factor alone draw you into marriage (1 Thess 4:3-5). When the overall biblical teaching on marriage is understood, it is quite clear that a number of factors besides eros need to line up before marriage is recommended.

If you are in a relationship where sexual attraction is especially intense, I cannot urge you strongly enough to make every effort to keep your head in thinking through the possibility of marriage. Err on the side of caution in allowing adequate time to get acquainted. Look at the other compatibility factors, and carefully consider how well you match up at these points. Also, seek out a qualified counselor and meet with that person individually and then together. Thoroughly explore with him or her the question of how fully compatible for marriage you actually are.

It is certainly possible that you will discover that you match up well at other points besides the physical. The fact that you are strongly attracted physically does not in itself recommend against marriage any more than it recommends for it. However, if you find that your overall compatibility is not strong enough to recommend marriage, you will need to take one of the most difficult steps anyone ever has to take. You will need to decide either not to go ahead with marriage or at least to shelve that possibility until your relationship has the chance to grow and season in other areas. As painful as that choice will be, it will be far less painful than entering a lifetime union that cannot possibly deliver what it seems to promise.

Ten

....

Are You Intellectually Compatible?

I WENT THROUGH A PHASE AS A YOUNG CHRISTIAN IN WHICH I assumed that the woman I married should be a musical performer like myself. I was director of a music ministry at the time, and so much of my life was wrapped up in this work that it seemed hard to imagine being married to someone without the same level of involvement in it. This assumption limited my options considerably, to say the least.

A wise older friend one day suggested that my marriage might be happier and more balanced if my wife did *not* share my intensive interest in music. I look back on that conversation now as one of the most important turning points in my thinking about marriage, for it broadened my thinking and opened me to new possibilities.

While Evie, whom I married several years later, did have a background in music education, she wasn't a performer, and our interests in music were quite different. I discovered the truth of my friend's advice during the first year of marriage, for coming home provided a welcome retreat from the fast-lane environment of the music ministry. With Evie I was able to turn off the stresses of the work and return to it refreshed. I suspect this wouldn't have happened as well had I been married to another performer.

Like other areas of compatibility which we're looking at, intellectual compatibility is one where our thinking easily gets clouded by myth and unreasonable ideals. While intellectual compatibility between a husband and wife is clearly important, defining what constitutes it in a given relationship is a delicate question. In my own case it was necessary to let go of an unfortunate assumption before I could find a truly compatible relationship.

I find Christians today obsessed with the concern for intellectual compatibility in marriage. While I'm sure this has always been a factor among those thinking about marriage, there are two trends which make this a unique obsession of our time. One is the rise in educational level and professional standing among women. If you look at marriages of those a generation or two before you, you find many examples of happy marriages in which the husband is college-educated, even with multiple degrees, while the wife never went beyond high school. Because the cultural pattern encouraged education and professional advancement among men and discouraged it among women, intellectual equality in marriage was not a major issue.

Today, of course, the cultural tide has changed considerably. While sexism remains a problem at times, women generally are encouraged to strive for their full potential and feel under considerable pressure to do so. As the lines of distinction between men and women become blurred in more and more educational and professional areas, both men and women come more and more to expect the person they marry to be their intellectual and creative match.

The other factor which makes intellectual compatibility a greater concern is the later age at which people tend to marry. It has become much more acceptable to be a professional single, especially in urban areas, and many purposely choose to delay marriage until they have finished their education and launched their career. Though this contributes to greater maturity at the time of marriage, it also makes the matter of finding a compatible relationship more challenging, at least from the standpoint of expectations. With each year of life your wisdom and experience grows, and while this is a wonderful benefit in itself, it also means that there are fewer of the opposite sex available who share your level of knowledge and accomplishment.

Equality Versus Compatibility

But while intellectual compatibility is a commendable goal in choosing a marriage partner, the challenge is not to define too rigidly what it must mean. The sort of arrangement that makes for healthy intellectual compatibility—the mix of personalities and aptitudes and gifts—in fact varies greatly from relationship to relationship and from marriage to marriage. But to find this arrangement, it will be necessary to let go of the notion that your mate must be your intellectual equal.

God has so constructed us that there are no two individuals on earth who are perfectly equal at any point of potential. Each has certain potentials which the other lacks. The closer you look the greater the differences become. And comparison is always an apples-and-oranges matter.

In addition, it's impossible to predict the direction which individual growth will take in a marriage. Like those who put an unreasonably high premium on sexual attraction, those who insist on an extreme level of intellectual equality with their spouse set themselves up for disappointment. In time they discover that their personal growth takes place at different speeds, and life takes their creative interests in different directions.

When Evie and I married twenty-seven years ago, neither of us had much idea that I would develop a strong interest in writing. Yet today writing is my most enjoyable creative outlet. While Evie enjoys reading my finished product, she has little interest or patience with the ponderous details of making ideas work out on paper, a task that engages all of my creative energy. Evie, on the other hand, has developed considerable skill in teaching music to children. She began working full-time as an elementary school music teacher ten years ago, and for the past nine years she has directed an elementary choir at our church. While I enjoy watching her work, I haven't been able to develop the passionate interest that has spurred her on and continues to inspire her to take every special seminar on elementary music she can possibly attend.

Our situation is typical of most marriages. Creative interests do tend to run in different directions as the years go on. In our case this hasn't been a problem, for we didn't begin marriage with the expectation that all our interests must be identical or that we must maintain some illusive notion of intellectual equality. Marriages where these expectations run high are threatened by such diversity.

What, then, should we be looking for in the way of intellectual compatibility with another person? Here the important thing is first to understand what the underlying needs really are that we're hoping will be met through intellectual compatibility—then to look at how well a relationship meets these. First, we hope that marriage will bring mental stimulation to our life. In short, we want the relationship to be *interesting*. Indeed, boredom is perhaps our greatest fear in entering marriage. Second, we want the marriage to be an environment where we are encouraged and challenged to realize our full potential, professionally and in other areas. We want our partner to believe in us and spur us on to develop our important gifts. When looked at from this angle, it becomes clear that a wide variety of relationship mixes can fulfill these needs.

Different Models of Intellectual Compatibility

Jerry and Alicia are both teachers in a large city high school; Jerry teaches biology and Alicia teaches chemistry. They met nearly fifteen years ago when both showed up to help with a student Christian fellowship group that met after school. They were quickly struck with the similarity of their interests in student ministry as well as their common professional and academic goals. They married a year later.

While Jerry and Alicia both greatly enjoy teaching, they find the public school environment stressful, the breakdown in discipline abhorrent and the work load burdensome. Their mutual involvement in this profession is a continual source of strength and renewal for both of them. The similarity of their subjects, too, allows for frequent interaction on material and lesson plans. They are both strong academics who enjoy long periods of study in their fields. If one wants to spend an evening or a weekend afternoon quietly reading, the other is usually quite amenable and joins in. The time often ends with a stimulating discussion of what each has learned.

Jerry and Alicia recognize that even if either should leave the teaching profession, that person would still continue to be an empathetic support to the other. Few would argue that they are intellectually compatible and an enviable match for marriage.

Bill and Ellen are a quite different yet no less impressive example. Now in their late thirties, they've been happily married for over ten years. Ellen is a pediatrician with a successful practice in the suburbs of a midwestern city. Bill is a physical education instructor working in several local elementary schools. In certain respects Bill and Ellen are as different as day and night. Ellen is drawn to the world of medicine; she thrives on reading medical journals, attending seminars and long evening discussions with professional comrades. Her life revolves around her work, and she strives to stay on the growing edge of her profession. Bill's reading is limited to sports magazines and an occasional novel. While he enjoys discussions about physical fitness, he has no interest in the fine details of medical doctrine. He is, in short, not an academic person. His passion is engaged by competitive sports and the world of outdoor adventure.

In her younger years, until her mid-twenties, Ellen assumed she'd only be happy married to another medical professional. She had two serious relationships, one with a young family physician and one with a surgical intern. Yet as each became more serious she began to worry that the intensity of their common interest in medicine wouldn't make for a healthy marriage. The competitive spirit between them seemed too strong, and there wasn't enough balance of other interests. Also, Ellen longed to raise children and enjoy a reasonably normal family life. It seemed hard to imagine how two physicians addicted to their practices could keep the home fires burning.

Ellen and Bill met at a church social when she was twenty-eight and he was twenty-seven. Though Ellen instinctively liked Bill, she at first resisted his attempts at a dating relationship, fearing the differences between them were too great. She was won over, however, on a three-day ski trip with singles from their church. Ellen was impressed by Bill's sensitivity to her bungling efforts as a novice skier. He seemed to know exactly what to do to help her gain skill and confidence in a sport that frankly intimidated her. By the end of the trip she was showing competence on a small slope that surprised even a house instructor.

In the ensuing months Bill introduced Ellen to racquetball and tennis. When she could steal an hour from her practice, she enjoyed going to watch him coach elementary soccer or baseball teams. She was constantly impressed with his ability to motivate these young sports enthusiasts. Evenings with Bill were always enjoyable, too, and Ellen was intrigued with how much fun she had doing simple things with him—attending a movie or going for a milk shake at the Dairy Queen. Though their professional interests were miles apart, they always seemed to have plenty to talk about—dreams of life and family and a mutual interest in community affairs. For the first time Ellen had a relationship that was a diversion from her professional life rather than one that immersed her more in it, and the effect was therapeutic.

Ellen was mildly astonished, too, that Bill was never intimidated by her success or her close friendships with fellow professionals. He wanted her to succeed and realized she needed their support. Gradually Ellen came to realize that there was the kind of balance in her relationship with Bill that would make for good family life. Ten years of marriage have proven the truth of Ellen's conclusion.

Bill's skill with children has translated well into parenting. He has been an excellent father to their three children, finding more time and motivation for parenting than most fathers are able to muster. Ellen has continued to progress in her career, but she has also welcomed the refuge which family life provides from the stresses of her job. She describes her relationship with Bill as a magnet which pulls her away from her natural obsession with work. Bill has grown in his career as well and was recently offered a principalship.

Balancing Intellectual Compatibility with Other Factors

Bill and Ellen's example brings out two important cautions to keep in mind in weighing intellectual compatibility in a relationship. One is that *balance is as important as similarity.* God wants to use a marriage relationship not only to sharpen our strong points but to strengthen and compensate for our weak points. We need to look carefully at how the marriage will do both. The second point is that *we cannot expect our partner to be a savior who provides all of the inspiration for personal growth we will ever need.* We'll need to continue to draw stimulation from friendships and associations outside of the marriage as well.

Here, to be sure, there are considerable differences in need from individual to individual and from relationship to relationship. Some do best in a situation like Jerry and Alicia's, where similarities seem to outweigh differences. Others, though—especially those who are self-starters by nature—do quite well in an arrangement like Bill and Ellen's. And others fall somewhere between these extremes.

If you are in your thirties, forties or beyond and have made good strides in your career, you have at least proven one thing: You can grow in your profession without the aid of a marriage relationship. Therefore, you may not need as much intellectual stimulation from marriage as you think. Be open to other options and to how God may wish to complement your life as well as nurture it through marriage and family life.

Again, I'm not saying that intellectual compatibility is unimportant in considering marriage. We simply need to be careful of unreasonable ideals about it and to remember that there are other factors to weigh as well. If you can give a confident affirmative to each of the following four questions, then it's reasonable to say that your relationship is intellectually compatible.

1. Do you have enough common areas of interest to keep your relationship interesting? Even though you may have strongly divergent interests in some areas, are there enough common points of interest to give basis to a long-term relationship?

2. Do you have profound respect for each other's gifts and areas of potential? Are you motivated to support and encourage each other at these points, even if your gifts differ considerably? Are you each comfortable with your partner's having friendships or associations with others who can be a support system for professional or creative growth?

3. Do you each want to be challenged to grow through the other's strong points? Though you will not share every interest in common, are there ways in which you hope the other will challenge you to grow and realize new horizons? Ellen, for instance, benefited immensely from Bill's athletic interests, and Bill was helped by Ellen to better understand some of the medical aspects of sports training. There should be, in other words, some points of contact between your areas of competence and a mutual desire to benefit from them.

4. Do you communicate well in the areas that will be essential to your life together in marriage? Even though you might be in different worlds professionally or academically, is there good agreement on issues such as lifestyle and family relationships?

Of course when the questions are posed this way, it's not greatly different from asking, "Are you good friends?" In the end *friendship* is the true test of intellectual compatibility.

Does the Husband Have to Be Stronger Intellectually?

An important question remains, however, and that is whether God wills that the husband should always be the clear intellectual superior of the wife in the ideal Christian marriage. Popular Christianity generally assumes so, and many Christians are uncomfortable, in theory at least, with an arrangement like Bill and Ellen's. While the most common question raised to me by Christian men is whether it's okay to marry when physical attraction is short of overwhelming, the most common question raised by women is whether they should marry a man whom they perceive is less gifted than they are intellectually.

Given the considerable educational advantages which men had throughout biblical times, it can probably be said that the husband was the intellectual superior in most marriages. However, Scripture never says as a matter of principle that the husband must always be intellectually stronger than the wife. To the contrary, in the most extensive description of the characteristics of a good wife, Proverbs 31:10-31, the wife is pictured as more intellectually gifted than her husband at several points: she is skilled in crafts (v. 13), astute in business (v. 18), gifted in real estate negotiations (v. 16), a superb manager of domestic affairs (vv. 14-15, 21-22, 27) and a gifted teacher and counselor (v. 26). It is of particular interest that her husband is not threatened by these qualities but instead praises her (vv. 28-29).

Just as God creates distinctive individuals, so there are distinctive marriages. To say it differently: *there are many different models for a healthy Christian marriage.* While some individuals will only be fulfilled in a traditional arrangement, many women and men are secure enough in themselves and in their relationship with Christ to function quite well in a marriage where the woman is more gifted intellectually, creatively or vocationally.

In many healthy relationships it will simply be impossible to say who is the intellectual superior. Both will have their own gifts, strengths and weaknesses. The wife may have a more glamorous career. Yet the husband, like Bill, may be gifted with athletic or social skills that give him special advantages in parenting. The possibilities and combinations are endless.

In marriages in which the wife clearly has the jump professionally, financially, creatively or intellectually, there will be some concessions to be made. The belief that the man should prevail at these points runs deep in our culture and may be a more significant part of your subconscious attitude toward marriage than you realize. You may have to adjust to the fact that your life together will take on a different pattern than you had long imagined would be the case in marriage. The sharing of responsibilities will probably break the conventional mold—the man will be expected to handle some domestic chores which tradition assigns to the wife. And there may be family members or friends who don't fully accept your arrangement or believe it is a truly Christian model for marriage.

All of these tradeoffs are well worth making, if your motivation for marriage is great enough, your compatibility is strong, and you are entering marriage with your eyes fully open to the concessions necessary. The important question is not how your relationship meshes with popular ideas of the ideal Christian marriage, but whether it fits God's design for your life and that of your partner. Will it bring out the best in both of you and contribute to your growth in Christ? If so, then you have found a pearl of great price. If gaining this prize means selling off some outmoded expectations, that is not too great a price to pay.

Eleven

....

Are You Spiritually Compatible?

MARRIAGES BETWEEN NONBELIEVERS CAN BE QUITE HAPPY AND successful in many ways. Christians, however, can enjoy fulfillment and fruitfulness in marriage that goes well beyond what others are able to experience. Because of their common bond in Christ they have the potential for marriage that is most uniquely blessed and used by God.

Since spiritual compatibility is essential to this happening, it is in many ways our greatest need in marriage. Yet two cautions must be borne in mind. One is that spiritual compatibility is not a panacea covering all potential problems in marriage. Some Christians do place too much weight on it. It sometimes happens that two people with a similar spiritual heritage (both from the same church or fellowship, for instance) or a similar commitment to Christian work (both planning to be missionaries) decide to marry without assessing their compatibility in other areas carefully enough. They assume that because both are Christians, conflicts will be transcended and the Lord will take care of all the problems that arise. Yet in time they discover that their differences at certain points are so great as to make life together very difficult.

Here the problem comes in thinking that spiritual compatibility is all that God is concerned about in a relationship. In reality Christ is Lord of our whole life—physical, emotional, social, mental, as well as spiritual. He creates each of us with different needs in these areas, and all of them should be weighed carefully in considering marriage. My purpose in treating spiritual compatibility in the midst of our list rather than at the top of it is to emphasize that it must not be considered in isolation from other areas.

The other caution is that we must be careful not to define spiritual compatibility too narrowly. Christians sometimes equate it too strongly with similarities in spiritual lifestyle, doctrinal belief or Christian vocation. Thus they can be too quick to think they are spiritually compatible with someone who

☐ belongs to the same church, fellowship or denomination
☐ has similar tastes in worship
☐ follows similar devotional practices
☐ is equally knowledgeable about Scripture
☐ has the same spiritual gifts
☐ has similar goals for personal ministry
☐ is equally expressive about spiritual matters

By the same token they may be too quick to think they are incompatible with someone who doesn't measure up to their expectations at these points. These things, though, often have little to do with whether two people are truly compatible spiritually. We must be careful not to major in minors here. Certain essentials are indispensable to a healthy spiritual relationship—points of agreement that must not be lightly brushed over. Beyond these there is much room for diversity on more peripheral matters. How much difference can be tolerated—even enjoyed—depends on the temperamental makeup of the two people. Yet the crucial question is how you agree on the essentials. The rest is often negotiable.

The Essentials of Spiritual Compatibility
What, then, are the essentials of spiritual compatibility in Christian marriage?

1. A common commitment to Christ as Lord and Savior. If Christ has become Lord of your life, it is unthinkable that he would lead you to marry someone without a common dedication to him. Invariably you would find yourself in the untenable position of serving two masters, in conflict over whether to please Christ or your spouse. And you'd deprive yourself for a lifetime of the chance to share the most significant part of your life with your most intimate earthly friend.

Yes, you may win your spouse to Christ. That does happen. Yet in most cases it doesn't. And too often a spouse is tempted to feign an interest in spiritual things simply to please his or her partner. You shouldn't consider marrying someone who hasn't first given their life to Christ in sincerity and then had the opportunity to put down some roots in him.

To this end Scripture commands, "Be ye not unequally yoked together with unbelievers" (2 Cor 6:14 KJV). While scholars argue over whether Paul had marriage in mind in this statement, it is unimaginable that a relationship as binding as marriage wouldn't fall within his boundaries of concern here. The imagery in being unequally yoked is profound and helpful to keep in mind—a horse and ox attached to the same cart and attempting to pull it at different paces are simply not effective.

Even more profoundly, Paul speaks elsewhere of the relationship between husband and wife in terms of the highest analogy he can muster—that of Christ and the church (Eph 5:21-33). The analogy makes little sense if both in the marriage are not Christian. There is a spiritual dimension in marriage which is at the heart of compassion and unity between husband and wife yet only fully possible when both know the Lord.

2. A similar view of biblical authority. Though I'm an evangelical with a firm stand on biblical infallibility, my teaching ministry brings me into many different Christian communions. I recognize that good marriages occur among Christians with varying views of biblical authority. The important thing is that husband and wife are reasonably unified in their perspective on this fundamental issue.

The problems that can occur were brought home to me by Jeff and Carolyn, a Christian couple whom I counseled. At first I was impressed by their strong compatibility at important points. Both were adventuresome individuals with a high commitment to social service, and each seemed to have a genuine concern for the other's welfare. Yet Carolyn looked upon the Bible, as I do, as a completely reliable source of God's will for our lives. While Jeff had a respect for Scripture, his view was more liberal and quite tenacious at that; he believed that Scripture should guide our thinking but not be the final authority. The result was that they came out at widely different points on several issues that were important to both of them, and those differences put unfortunate stress on their relationship. As there seemed little hope of reconciling these opinions, I recommended with regret that they shouldn't marry.

What we're speaking of here, of course, is only common sense. Unless you and your partner are working from the same set of instructions, the possibility of conflict is simply too great. Without a unified view of biblical authority, you'll likely find yourselves unequally yoked at more points than would be tolerable in a healthy marriage.

3. A similar understanding of biblical values that are important to family life. Similar views on biblical authority, however, do not guarantee identical interpretations of Scripture. Evangelicals with a high view of Scripture, for instance, come out at different points on the issue of male and female roles in marriage. Whatever your viewpoints on this matter, it's vital that you are in agreement. The question of what priority should be given to family life over church involvement and career is another area where Christians arrive at different points based on different interpretations of Scripture. Again, the important thing is to be of one heart and mind on this central issue.

You and your partner should each be clear about which spiritual and moral values are important to you individually—so important that they are nonnegotiable in marriage. You then need to be certain that there is agreement on these points before you go ahead with marriage. Often the help of a third party in sorting them through is beneficial.

4. Extremely important! A desire to continue growing in Christ. As vital as unity is on these key points, it's just as important that each of you desire to continue growing in your relationship with Christ. Without this desire, your spiritual life—individually and together—will stagnate. And without it, sensitivity to differences in each other's perspectives will be hard to come by. The urge for spiritual growth is critical both to personal spiritual health and to the vitality of the relationship.

These four essentials are vital to a healthy Christian marriage. When they are present, differences can often be tolerated, or even enjoyed, at other points of spiritual perspective. It depends greatly on the personalities of the two people. Some will need a high level of similarity at most points related to spiritual life. Others who are secure enough in their relationship with Christ will thrive and grow through certain differences in spiritual perspective. I've even seen occasional instances where healthy marriages exist with husband and wife attending different churches. Though this isn't normally an ideal arrangement, it shouldn't be categorically ruled out as never acceptable in Christian marriage.

Just recently a Christian woman told me about her own upbringing in a family where the father and mother were active in different denominations. The parents respected each other's positions, yet were open in talking with the children about their differences. She felt strongly that the experience broadened her and her four siblings, making deeper relationships with Christ possible.

Male Headship

As with intellectual compatibility, we come here to the question of male and female roles. What about the traditional view of male headship? Is it necessary for the husband always to be spiritually stronger than the wife and the clear spiritual leader in the relationship?

Many Christians would say yes. Yet we encounter a statistical problem: There are more mature Christian women than men both within the body of Christ as a whole and in most local churches and fellowships. Does this mean that only those women who are fortunate enough to form a bond with a man who is their undisputed spiritual superior are entitled to marry?

Here it is important to understand what Scripture teaches and what it doesn't. Scripture declares that the husband is head of the wife as Christ is head of the church and that the husband is to love his wife as Christ loves the church (Eph 5:23, 25). The wife in turn is to submit herself to her husband as to Christ and to respect her husband (Eph 5:22-33). Yet Scripture leaves it fairly open as to how the dynamics of this interaction can take place in a given relationship. Again we come back to the fact of different models for a healthy Christian marriage.

Many Christians get locked into certain stereotyped ideas of what male headship must mean in marriage. It's often assumed that the man must have greater spiritual knowledge, be more assertive in matters such as encouraging Bible study, family devotion and church attendance, and in general be a sharper spiritual personality. Yet while some will need these traditional dynamics in their relationship, Scripture doesn't lock us into such stereotypical roles.

God looks more upon the heart than he does upon a person's outward spiritual sharpness or accumulation of spiritual knowledge. I've counseled with several couples considering marriage in which the man simply hasn't had the same advantages for spiritual growth which the woman has had. In one case the woman (Jenny, twenty-nine) belonged to a strong InterVarsity chapter in college and since graduating had been active in a thriving singles ministry of a large, dynamic evangelical church. The man (John, twenty-eight) came to Christ in college through a campus ministry. Then he joined the navy and served in locales where good spiritual nurture simply wasn't available. When I counseled with them, he was stationed at a remote base without a strong church within driving distance.

Jenny had the clear advantages of background here. She was considerably more knowledgeable of Scripture, more comfortable in Christian gatherings and in initiating spiritual matters with John. Yet as I came to know each of them, I felt John's heart for Christ was every bit as strong as Jenny's. He was teachable and eager to grow. He was supportive of Jenny and not intimidated by her spiritual strength. Because in general he was a mature and congenial individual, and since Jenny strongly respected him, I recommended they marry.

An important part of male headship is supporting the wife at her points of strength. It is commonly thought that male headship means lording it over the wife in spiritual matters. Yet the husband is called to love his wife as Christ loves the church. It must be remembered that Christ's lordship over the church involves a strongly submissive role (in John 13, for instance, where he washes the disciples' feet), and that Christ loves the church by giving gifts to its members and encouraging them to develop and use them. He even said that his followers in some respects would do greater works than he had done (Jn 14:12).

Part of male headship, then, involves respecting the wife's gifts and encouraging her in their development. In every marriage there is a unique mix of gifts, strengths and weaknesses. In some it will happen that the wife has a stronger gift for spiritual leadership or teaching. If the husband supports and encourages her, and she respects him for his points of strength, it can still be said that the reality of Ephesians 5:21-33 is being worked out. Again, it is of interest that in the six references to Priscilla and Aquila in the New Testament, she is mentioned first in four of them (Acts 18:18, 26; Rom 16:3; 2 Tim 4:19). Apparently she was generally regarded as the stronger individual spiritually.

While Paul uses different spiritual metaphors to depict the role of husband and wife, his overriding concern is that husband and wife be mutually submitted to one another. Thus he begins his discussion of husband and wife relations in Ephesians 5 by declaring, "Submit to one another out of reverence for Christ" (a verse that is often omitted in traditional discussions of male-female roles). In 1 Corinthians 7:4 he makes the same point regarding the physical relationship in marriage: "The wife's body does not belong to her alone but also to her husband. In the same way, the husband's body does not belong to him alone but also to his wife." The concept of mutual submission implies that either husband or wife may have an authority role at different points in the marriage. Paul is clearly not suggesting a rigid pattern of hierarchy but a situation where there will be a lot of give-and-take.

Beyond Male Headship

While many Christians follow a straightforward interpretation of Paul's teachings, some believers with a high view of biblical authority conclude that headship was not meant to be binding for Christians of all times.[1] It is thought that such teaching was intended to correct some unfortunate circumstances in the early churches or as an acquiescence to the culture of that time. Wives were told to submit to their husbands so that Christians would not challenge a social custom in a way that would hinder the spread of the gospel. In the same way Christian women were instructed to wear veils and not to talk during worship.

These commands, it is argued, should be seen in the same class as those about slaves obeying their masters. They had their place in the culture of the first century. But just as we would not look upon slavery as God's perfect will, neither should we insist on male headship in marriage as God's ideal. God's highest design for marriage is reflected in Galatians 3:28, where Paul says, "There is neither Jew nor Greek, slave nor free, male nor female, for you are all one in Christ Jesus." The unity portrayed in that passage should be understood as touching all aspects of life, not simply the spiritual, and has important bearing on the marriage relationship.

If you believe that Paul's commands on male-female roles in marriage were culturally conditioned, then of course you will not feel constrained to follow the tradition of the husband's being the stronger spiritual personality in marriage. You will understand the New Testament as allowing latitude on this matter, while still encouraging mutual respect, love and spiritual maturity within the marriage relationship. But even the straightforward reading of Paul's teachings brings us to the same conclusion once the full breadth of his thinking is understood.

Paul seems more intent on encouraging mutual submission and partnership in marriage than on forming a rigid pattern of spiritual roles. In the end, whichever interpretive approach you take to Scripture, you come out at virtually the same point—that there are different possibilities for the spiritual maturity mix between husband and wife. The vital matter is that each be intent upon following and growing in Christ and upon being a redemptive spiritual companion to the other.

Twelve

· · · · · · · · · · ·

Are You Emotionally Compatible?

WHEN NATHAN AND CECILIA MARRIED, THEY HAD HIGH HOPES OF working together in ministry. With Nathan's seminary training and Cecilia's experience in church education, they seemed an ideal match. They married shortly after Nathan graduated and immediately accepted a call to pastor a fledgling church in New England.

After four years under their leadership, the church had grown from fewer than fifty members to over two hundred. Cecilia and Nathan were well accepted and loved by these people, and both worked tirelessly. Enthusiasm ran high in this young flock, which already was taking steps toward building its first facility on a piece of land donated by a generous member.

Given these factors, Cecilia was astonished when Nathan suggested they consider accepting an offer to begin a new church in Kansas City. She couldn't imagine quitting a situation that was going so well, and the thought of leaving these people who depended on them so greatly smacked of desertion. Nathan was equally astonished that Cecilia couldn't understand his enthusiasm for this new adventure. And far from thinking of leaving as desertion, Nathan felt their present church would benefit from fresh blood. "We've done our job here," he insisted. "We've gotten the fire burning, but it's time for someone else to come in and fan the flame."

For several weeks the issue brought them to an impasse whenever it came up, and tension mounted. Finally they agreed to meet with a denominational counselor and let him advise them what to do. After three sessions, the counselor concluded: "I simply cannot tell you which direction to go. Both are equally justified. What you're dealing with here is a fundamental difference in personality. Nathan by his very nature is motivated to seek variety and new adventure. Cecilia has a need to nurture situations that are already successful. You'll do best to honestly face your differences and seek a compromise."

Distinctive Motivations

Nathan and Cecilia's example brings us to the heart of another compatibility issue which we need to look at—*emotional compatibility*. We're reminded of the sorts of conflicts that can occur when two people are motivated in basically different ways.

Scripture attests that God fashions each of our lives with a unique motivational pattern. The result is that our natural emotional responses to the events of life are different. We each instinctively enjoy certain types of activities and incline toward certain tastes. Our personal judgments of what is best for us and even of more fundamental questions of right and wrong are strongly affected by our motivational pattern. This pattern is at the heart of what is meant by personality, or our unique psychological orientation to life.[1]

The idea that God gives distinctive personality is not well accepted by all believers. Many equate personality with the old nature which has been erased by Christ. Scripture, though, never comes close to such a spiritualized concept of personality. To the contrary, Psalm 139:13 declares that God creates our "inward parts," a term used by the Hebrews to signify the personality or distinctive emotional life of a person.[2] Paul, too, speaks to this idea in 1 Corinthians 12:4-6, where he notes that God endows each of us with distinctive *working*, which in the Greek means "energizing" or "motivation."

What does the New Testament mean, then, when it says that we who have been born of Christ have a new nature? It is crucial to understand that when the New Testament speaks of our new nature in Christ, it is not referring to the annulment of our personality but its *redirection*. The two natures refer to different allegiances for our personality. Under the old nature I resist God's will, while under the new nature I joyfully respond to it. Yet it is still my own unique personality which responds in either case. Thus we find hundreds of examples throughout Scripture of individuals doing the will of God from their hearts but in their own highly distinctive ways. Our individual personalities are the stamp of God's image upon us.[3]

The Significance of Personality in Choosing a Mate

Each of us will do well to take what steps we can to understand our personality. There are few areas where the ancient adage "know thyself" more clearly applies. Through understanding the motivational tendencies that are most fundamental to our being, we gain a treasured insight into how God has designed our life — and what he wants us to do with it.

Having said that, it must also be said that we can exaggerate the significance of the personality factor in choosing a mate. The idea of matching personality types has become quite faddish in recent years and a near obsession in some circles. Pop theories abound, promising to unfold the hidden mysteries of your personality through analysis of some single factor (everything from blood types to birth order to "colors" of your personality to signs in the Zodiac is claimed to hold the key). Then they will tell you with prophetic certainty what personality type you must match with to assure a happy marriage. Each theory contends that certain personality combinations are destined for success in marriage, others for failure.

A simple look around you, though, reveals the lie in this extreme notion. You don't have to look far to find examples of virtually every combination of personalities imaginable existing together in happy marriages. It's not hard, either, to find examples of couples who seem well-matched personality-wise yet have not done well in marriage. Common sense tells us that personality doesn't hold some mystical key to success or failure in marriage.

The fact is that there are inherent strengths and weaknesses to any combination of two personalities in a marriage relationship. Any mix of personality types can work well in marriage if both individuals are mature and compatible at other points. Likewise, any combination, even the most seemingly compatible, can be dis-astrous if other factors don't line up well.

There is considerable benefit to understanding each other's personalities, to be sure. But the value comes in helping you understand where your potential for conflict will lie rather than in giving you a magical answer about whether to marry. It shouldn't be thought that personality is some esoteric factor beyond others we're looking at which might annul or confirm a decision to marry.

Nathan and Cecilia's conflict, for instance, didn't prove that their personalities were poorly matched for marriage. In fact, these two were highly compatible. What their conflict revealed was that they didn't understand their personality differences well enough. They should have gone into marriage with a clearer understanding of their different motivational patterns. As they came to appreciate these differences, they were quite willing to make adjustments, and this is what compatibility is all about. (Their solution: Stay another year at the New England church, then look for a new opportunity; commit themselves to a five-year term with any church they serve in the future.)

My advice to couples considering marriage is first to weigh the other compatibility factors we're looking at. Do you feel significant compassion for each other? Is your friendship strong? Is the sexual attraction strong enough to justify marriage? Are you intellectually and spiritually compatible in ways that are important to both of you? Then look carefully at how your expectations match at important points (discussed in the next chapter). Finally, carefully consider whether you are both ready for a lifetime commitment. Do you have good evidence to support your conclusion?

At this point you should have sufficient information to make a wise and confident decision about marriage. If you choose to marry, then look more closely at your personality differences. Take a test or work through an exercise together. Talk about the results or discuss them with a professional counselor or trusted friend. Note where the strengths and weaknesses in your relationship lie. Look carefully at where adjustments and compromises will be needed.

But determine in advance that you will be willing to make these adjustments, even before you know what they must be. If you care deeply for the other person and are mature enough for marriage, you *will* be willing. Don't let the results of personality analysis, which are always highly subjective and never completely reliable, deter you from going ahead with marriage if you are otherwise convinced that you should—or convince you to marry if you are otherwise uncertain. Simply take these results as a further help toward entering marriage with your eyes open.

Understanding Each Other's Motivational Pattern

What are specific steps you can take to better understand your personalities? Any standardized personality test, offered through a church, counseling service or college vocational center can serve the purpose, provided you both take the same test and have competent instruction on interpreting the results.

If you prefer to do this without outside help, let me suggest a simple and enjoyable exercise.[4] Pick a quiet setting and a time when you are both relaxed and free from other pressures. First, decide together on a method for classifying personalities. If you are not already familiar with a particular approach, you can use the traditional Hippocratic model. While limited, it does provide a track to run on and makes for good discussion. Even Christian psychiatrist Paul Tournier insists that with all of its limitations, this "classification . . . is still the best. Proof of this is that with only minor variations numerous authors make what is basically the same classifications into types."[5] It recognizes four prominent personality types:

☐ *the choleric*—inclined toward action, leadership, change, getting things done

☐ *the sanguine*—inclined toward feeling, empathy

☐ *the melancholic*—inclined toward thinking, analysis

☐ *the phlegmatic*—inclined toward maintaining order, accepting things as they are[6]

Be certain that both of you are in clear agreement about what these terms mean. Then spend thirty minutes silently reflecting on your lives, with pen and paper handy to write down your thoughts. Try to identify the experiences that have been most successful or meaningful to you, from early childhood to the present. Think of this as an ink-blot test—your first impressions count the most. Write a one-sentence description of each important accomplishment that comes to mind. Note the experiences that were important to you, whether or not you think anyone else was impressed with them. What comes to mind may be anything from running a successful lemonade stand when you were five to passing algebra in eighth grade to getting your Ph.D. at thirty. Try to come up with twenty to thirty examples each.

When you finish, give your lists to each other. Then allow fifteen minutes for each to reflect silently on the other's responses. Regard these responses as a map to your partner's motivational pattern. Try to determine what the most basic personality characteristic is that underlies the accomplishments which he or she has listed as important. Do they seem to indicate a desire to lead, for instance (choleric)? To probe for deeper understanding (melancholic)? To enjoy life (sanguine)? To make life more orderly (phlegmatic)? Finally, drawing on your conclusion and on all other knowledge that you have of your partner, list the personality categories in the order that you think best describes her or him (choleric-phlegmatic-sanguine-melancholic, for instance). Then share your conclusions with each other.

Of course, allow the other a fair hearing if he or she thinks your description is inaccurate. Listen carefully to the reasons, and if necessary revise your description. But realize that if your opinions vary widely, the truth probably lies somewhere between the extremes.

Finally, accept your descriptions of each other as, while imperfect, at least a track to run on and a basis for discussing the dynamics of your relationship in marriage. Look honestly at where the strengths and weaknesses in your relationship are likely to lie. Note especially how the dominant thrusts in your personalities are likely to influence the way you respond to life and to each ocher.

How Different Personalities Interact

While you probably won't find it difficult to identify strengths and weaknesses in your personality mix, once you understand your individual motivational patterns, some examples of how the classic personality types interact may help. Again, I draw on these for the sake of simplicity, realizing that no one perfectly matches any of these ideal types.

A *choleric-choleric* relationship produces a marriage with very strong leadership potential. If you agree on your goals, you'll stoke each other's fire considerably and be a great service to those with whom you work. Yet the potential for butting heads in this combination is also great. Lots of compassion and patience with each other will be needed.

When the choleric personality combines with any other type, the choleric brings leadership and motivational strength to the relationship. The choleric can inspire the sanguine, melancholic or phlegmatic to set goals and to break the inertia tendencies to which each of these types is vulnerable. Likewise, each of these can have a redemptive influence on the choleric. The sanguine can deepen the feeling capacity of the choleric; the melancholic can help the choleric to approach life more thoughtfully, and the phlegmatic can inspire needed patience, caution and organizational skills. Yet the choleric can be impatient with the changeable emotions of the sanguine, the analytical spirit of the melancholic or the meticulousness of the phlegmatic. Likewise, each of these can be intolerant of the choleric's high energy approach to life and the obsession with achievement and goals.

A *sanguine-sanguine* combination can produce a highly empathetic marriage, one that is capable of showing great compassion toward children and others. The danger in this combination is lack of discipline, as sanguines tend to get caught up in the emotions of the moment.

In a *sanguine-melancholic* relationship the empathetic sanguine can give needed emotional support to the melancholic's probing concerns. The sanguine can also help the melancholic to enjoy the moment and to break out of moodiness. The latter can help the sanguine to think as well as feel, to get beyond the grip of immediate feelings, and to see different sides of issues which the sanguine may tend to judge too quickly by instinct alone. The danger in this mix can be impatience—the sanguine with the ponderousness of the melancholic, the latter with the changeability of the sanguine. Also sanguines, with their highly empathetic nature, can get drawn into the melancholic's moodiness yet not be able to handle that state as well or derive the creative benefit from it which the melancholic often does.

In a *sanguine-phlegmatic* marriage the phlegmatic can bring discipline and order to the sanguine's potentially chaotic life, while the sanguine can help the phlegmatic to better recognize and experience feelings. Again, as in other mixes, patience and acceptance can be a challenge. The sanguine may regard the phlegmatic as too mechanical and chide the phlegmatic for being out of touch with feelings, while the latter may view the sanguine as fickle or capricious.

The obvious danger of a *melancholic-melancholic* relationship is moodiness and depression. Two melancholics may drag each other into such an analytical spirit that the practicalities of life are ignored. Yet important artistic and intellectual achievements are sometimes born of such relationships, and two melancholics can have a knack for inspiring each other to greater horizons. This arrangement can work well among two mature individuals.

A *melancholic-phlegmatic* arrangement can be excellent if each is accepting and respectful of the other's special gifts. The phlegmatic can help the melancholic with the personal organization that is so important to achieving his or her creative goals. The melancholic in turn can deepen the phlegmatic. Again, the potential for impatience and intolerance of each other's inclinations is obvious.

Finally, the *phlegmatic-phlegmatic* mix is of all the combinations the one least prone to conflict, for phlegmatics tend by nature to be more stoic and to enjoy the endless range of routine details necessary to maintaining a home and family life. Dangers inherent in this arrangement include boredom and insensitivity to the temperamental distinctions of children.

While there are beauty and special potential in any mix of two personalities, there are vulnerabilities and potential problems as well. Any of these combinations can work well among mature, compassionate individuals. Again, we are reminded that marriage is for adults—for those who regard their differences not as a threat but as an inspiration for growth, who are determined to negotiate their differences and who ultimately view the relationship as more important than their own individuality.

We are reminded, too, of the need for each partner to have friendships and associations, outside of the marriage, that inspire strength and growth at points where the marriage relationship is weak or vulnerable. While marriage is the most important human relationship we enter into, it can never be expected to meet all of our growth or companionship needs.

Thirteen

Are Your Expectations Compatible?

ONE SUNDAY EVENING AFTER CHURCH, WHEN I WAS A YOUNG Christian, I asked some friends to go with me to see an old musician friend perform in Waldorf, Maryland, about an hour's drive away. The place we were headed for was, to put it politely, a dive, and I assumed the others knew it.

A woman in the group asked if she could first stop by home to change her clothes. We dropped her off, then waited for her in the car for some time. Finally she emerged dressed fit to kill.

On the way someone finally mustered the courage to ask her why she was so finely dressed for the sort of establishment we were going to visit. Didn't she know there were no plush clubs in Waldorf? Astonished, she replied, "I thought you said we were going to *the* Waldorf."

The incident is a classic example of how false expectations arise. In this case I assumed that my friend knew exactly where we were going, while she of course drew a quite different conclusion from what I said.

On a much more serious level, the problem of differing expectations is a real one for two people entering marriage. All too often each person carries quite different assumptions about what life together will be like. Even when there is no attempt to deceive, each may develop certain expectations which are not understood or shared by the other. One may be expecting the Waldorf, while the other has a quite different idea in mind.

For this reason, it is extremely important that two people considering marriage spend considerable time discussing and comparing their expectations and looking honestly at how they are likely to mesh. As we've seen, congeniality and flexibility are vital factors in marriage. Yet even the most flexible person brings to marriage certain expectations that are inseparable from his or her idea of a successful marriage. I hope this chapter will challenge you to look carefully at how well your expectations match in areas that are important to you.

Significant Areas of Expectation

Male and female roles. Regardless of where you come out on the issue of male headship, there are still many practical questions about male and female roles that you will need to resolve. In *How to Choose the Wrong Marriage Partner and Live Unhappily Ever After,* Robert Mason and Caroline Jacobs list conflict over male-female roles first among twenty-eight factors likely to deteriorate a marriage.[1] I agree, as this issue has been a major factor in most Christian marriage breakups that I've witnessed.

I find that most often when there is conflict over male and female roles in a Christian marriage, the man entered marriage expecting a fairly traditional arrangement while the woman wanted greater freedom. Yet even couples who believe in equal partnership face many practical role questions which can cause conflict. Is the wife expected to work? If so, does she have the same freedom to pursue a career as the husband does? If children come along, will either be expected to cut back their work hours or in other ways carry greater responsibility for parenting? Who'll get up at 3:00 a.m. to change the diaper? And what about the endless range of domestic responsibilities—cooking, cleaning, maintaining the home and yard, paying bills and preparing to entertain guests? How will the burdens be divided?

My purpose is not to recommend one perspective on male and

female roles over another. Again, there are many workable models for a good marriage. The important matter is to agree on what *your* arrangement will be.

Educational goals. Frequently it's expected that one spouse will work to give the other the benefit of finishing college or graduate school. If so, is the other expected to return the favor once his or her program is completed? Be sure to have clear agreement on this question before marrying, for the potential for misunderstanding and hurt feelings here is great.

Standard of living. It's often argued that one should only marry someone from his or her same economic background. A woman who has grown up in a large home in the suburbs will not do well with a man from the inner city, for instance. In reality, marriages between those of different economic backgrounds sometimes work well, and of course marriages between those of similar backgrounds sometimes fizzle. Here expectations play a much greater role than past experience. A man from a poor family might have a perfectly happy marriage with a woman raised in Beverly Hills if they both have similar expectations for their lifestyle. By the same token, two people from similar backgrounds may have radically different aspirations for their future.

Of course flexibility about your economic future is essential. You can never predict how the financial tide will turn. Yet unless there is reasonable agreement between you about the standard of living you would like to achieve, the potential for conflict will be considerable.

While it is important to talk about your desires for your standard of living, it is just as important to be clear about your values. Are there moral, spiritual or ministry considerations which affect the way you think about your economic future? Don't assume that because both of you are Christians you will automatically be of one mind on this issue.

Some Christians believe that as a matter of principle they should keep their lifestyle as simple as possible, others that their standard of living should have a clearly defined upper limit, while others insist that you shouldn't place limits on the blessings

God may bestow on you. Christians vary, too, on the question of giving. How much of your income will you plan to give away? And what types of concerns will you give to?

Be sure that you have a clear understanding of each other's "wants" and "oughts." This is an area where your desires and values need to be in close agreement.

Vocational goals. Beyond questions of male and female roles, does either of you have a vocational goal which would affect family life in a way that would be unacceptable to the other? The man who wants to be a pastor may have a difficult marriage with a woman who puts a high premium on family privacy. The woman who wants to be a physician will need a husband who is highly tolerant of the erratic lifestyle involved.

Christians sometimes ask me whether the opportunity for marriage should ever be a reason for reconsidering your vocational goals. Suppose, for instance, that you've been planning to become a missionary but now have the opportunity to marry someone who isn't open to missionary service or to living in a different culture? Would you be selling out to change your career plans for the sake of marrying this person? (While this question is most frequently asked me by those entering missionary or ministry-related vocations, it's sometimes raised by others as well.)

My answer is that it depends upon the reasons underlying your career choice. Does this vocation seem to fit your gifts and your motivational pattern better than any other? Then you should only consider marrying someone who can be supportive of your vocational goals. If, however, you are less than certain about where your strongest gifts and motivations lie, you should feel free to stay flexible about your career direction. God could use the opportunity for marriage as much as any other circumstance to lead you or redirect you. Unfortunately, our Christian culture does not make it easy for you at this point. Some Christian groups place a high priority upon first resolving your vocational choice, then choosing a mate. If the one you want to marry is not open to your vocational goals, then find someone else ("master, mission, mate," as the adage goes).

Scripture, though, never constrains us to such a rigid chronology in our life's choices. When we consider the very high priority Paul places upon those who want to marry doing so when the opportunity is present (1 Cor 7), we must conclude that there are times when the choice of a mate should precede the choice of a vocation. It will vary from person to person, but we are not locked into an inflexible pattern.

We hear it taught, too, that God gives believers a "call"—a vocation they are locked into forever. Many assume that once they feel a strong inspiration to follow a certain vocation, from that point on they are not free to reconsider. However, such a moment of inspiration is usually a psychological experience giving you insight into your deepest desires and not a direct and binding message from God.[2] It is used by him to help you understand what you most want to do at the time, but it should not be taken as a permanent mandate. Your experience of inspiration is based upon your own understanding at that point—of yourself, of God, of opportunities in the world. As your understanding grows and changes, your sense of inspiration about what to do with your life may change also.

When we carefully examine Scripture on the point, we find that most of the time God guides not through a blinding revelation which tells you once and for all what he wants you to do for the rest of your life but incrementally, each day bringing new insight into his plan for your life. The opportunity for marriage can be a part of this process of enlightenment.

In any case, you shouldn't feel guilty for rethinking your career plans. You may or may not decide that the opportunity for marriage is a reason to change them. But you should at least feel free to consider the possibility.

Number of children and timing. Many entering marriage are quite happy to stay open on this question and let time and circumstance decide the family constellation. Others, though, have strong feelings about wanting a family of a certain size. And some are not eager to have children. Few issues are more important to talk through before marriage.

Relationship to in-laws. Will an in-law live with you? How much involvement with the spouse's family is expected? Expectations on this level can differ widely and be a considerable source of contention.

Social expectations. How public or private will your life together be? Does either of you feel strongly that you must be involved together as a couple in certain social activities, groups or relationships? Does one of you love to have guests over while the other longs for a quiet house and time alone?

Time together. How much premium do you each put on planned, private time together? Does either have a strong need for frequent, regular time set aside for being together alone as a couple?

Geographic expectations. Will you or your partner only be happy living in a certain geographical region or in a certain type of area—urban, country, suburban, ethnic, and so on?

Recreational desires and hobbies. Again, this is an area where many couples are highly flexible. But some do feel strongly that they and their spouse should be involved together in certain recreational activities. Don't take it for granted that you both agree about this—talk it through.

Make Your Own List

These are just some of the areas of expectation where flexibility or mutuality is most essential in marriage. I have suggested them partly to prime the pump. You can undoubtedly think of others that will be significant to your own marriage. I would, in fact, strongly encourage you each to make a list of all the important expectations that you hold for marriage. If you find that either of you has a strong expectation which isn't shared by the other and isn't negotiable, I would advise you not to marry unless this difference can be reconciled.

On the other hand, if your expectations align well at these points—or are truly flexible—you have another excellent indication of compatibility. If your relationship measures well in the other areas we've looked at, this is the final green light you need to make a confident decision to marry.

Fourteen

Finally Deciding

IF YOU ARE IN A SERIOUS RELATIONSHIP AND, WHILE READING THIS book, have been trying to decide whether to marry, it's possible you have already reached a decision. It may be that a single issue was holding you back, and it no longer seems so crucial. Or it may be that exploring the compatibility factors has enabled you to resolve the direction of your relationship.

Yet you may still be on the fence about what to do—fairly certain about marrying but not convinced enough to make a firm decision. This could mean that you need to allow more time for getting to know one another better. But it's also possible that you already do know everything you need to know—or are likely to be able to discover—to make a responsible decision about whether to marry.

Do all of the following apply to you?

☐ You and your partner are both at least twenty-five years old.

☐ Your relationship is already well into its second year or beyond.

☐ You have spent considerable time together during this period. In other words, this hasn't been a long-distance relationship; you've been together frequently and under a wide variety of circumstances.

☐ Your communication has been good.

☐ You have carefully weighed your compatibility at the important points, and you match up well. You are both mature enough for marriage. There are no major red flags.

☐ There is no significant extenuating circumstance yet to be resolved (such as career direction or a decision about education) that could have bearing on whether you decide to marry.

If you meet these criteria, then chances are good you are at a point where you can make a responsible decision about marriage. If you doubt you are actually there yet, then consider the following:

☐ What additional information could you gain that would allow you to make this decision with greater confidence?

☐ By waiting longer will you be in a better position to make an informed decision? Why?

☐ What else might be gained by delaying the decision?

If you are not able to give a good answer to any of these questions, then it's probable you already are in a position to make a responsible decision.

This is not to say that you should feel compelled to decide at this time. If both of you are comfortable letting the relationship continue undefined, then of course you should feel free to stay uncommitted. Yet if your partner is convinced about marriage and eager to go ahead, then you may owe it to him or her to take steps to try to resolve your own feelings. This is particularly true if you're already at least fairly convinced, yet still feel the need for some final confirmation. If this is your situation, then I highly recommend that you take two further steps.

Get Counsel

First, select at least three people whom you respect and ask them if they will meet with you to advise you about your decision. Though a group meeting can have its advantages, you will probably do best to meet separately with each person. At least two of these advisers should be married individuals with some years in an established happy marriage, and of course it's fine to meet with a couple. If you have a good relationship with your own parents, include them. Including your pastor or a professional counselor is often a good idea as well.

Request specifically to meet with each person for an hour, and select an unhurried time and a setting where you're not likely to be interrupted. When you meet, give the person some background on your relationship (if he or she is not already familiar with it), and explain what you see to be the pros and cons of marrying. Ask them to tell you if they see further issues you should consider. Then ask them, if they are willing, to venture their opinion on whether you should marry or not.

One reason you may resist doing this is because you fear that others won't really want to help you. You feel that you're intruding on their time, and if they agree to meet with you, it will only be reluctantly. Let me assure you that most people greatly enjoy giving advice and are flattered to be asked for it, particularly with a decision as important as marriage. I think you'll find most not only willing, but quite happy to talk with you. Even very busy pastors find it refreshing to deal with an issue as enjoyable as marriage in the midst of the more distressing concerns that often absorb their time. (My only advice is to be specific about requesting an hour, and don't let the meeting drag on beyond that time. If the other person wants to extend it, fine, but let him or her take the initiative.)

Another reason you may hesitate to seek counsel is the fear that others will spiritualize the issues and not deal directly with your concerns. You may fear getting a response like, "Don't worry, you'll have perfect peace when it's time to go ahead." Or "Just let the Lord show you in his own way and time what to do." You may even fear that they will make you feel silly for approaching the marriage decision as an issue, rather than simply waiting for clear spiritual guidance.

If you do unwittingly end up with persons who spiritualize, graciously thank them for their insight—for they may be responding from the most compassionate and reverent motives—but move on and look for someone who is willing to address the issues more directly. Above all, don't let one who spiritualizes lay a guilt trip on you for taking a more practical approach to your decision. You are being every bit as spiritual as they are. You are simply seeking to obey the Lord's command to use the mind he has given you for making responsible decisions.

There are many people who will give you a thoughtful and sensitive response. They will readily appreciate the issues you're wrestling with and be more than happy to talk them through with you. The key is to be careful whom you choose to counsel you.

In terms of evaluating the advice you receive, you should resist the temptation to think that any person is giving you the final answer about what to do. It is particularly tempting to think this if he or she is a spiritual authority whom you highly revere, a parent or someone with a strong personality. Yet while you should respect their counsel and weigh it carefully, you should take the counsel as *advice*, not prophecy. Remember that the value of counsel in the biblical understanding is not to give you a crystal-ball insight into God's will but to stimulate your thinking—to stretch you to think more deeply and clearly about an issue, to notice new alternatives and see old ones in a new light. In the end it remains your responsibility before God to make your own decision. Even if what you decide to do differs from what anyone has advised, you have still benefited greatly from the process of getting counsel.

Of course, if all of your counselors advise you to do the same thing (to marry or not to marry), then there's a good possibility this is the course you should follow. The burden of proof is more strongly upon you now to show why you shouldn't go in this direction. Yet sometimes the burden of proof can be met, and Scripture is full of examples where one person was right against the multitude. The important thing is to have a clear reason for what you decide. Clear-minded thinking should be your goal.

Usually, getting advice from a multitude (or at least a small multitude) of counselors will help you greatly toward this end.

Taking a Personal Retreat

After you have talked your decision through with several people, I recommend that you take a personal retreat. My conviction about the value of such retreats springs from my own experience as much as anything. It was on a one-and-a-half-day silent retreat in the winter of 1973 that I first realized that I really did want to marry Evie. It took some uncluttered time for me to sort it all through, and the return on that very small investment of time has been indescribable.

By "personal retreat" I mean a period of time set aside for being alone with the Lord to pray and think through your decision. I recommend investing at least one full day in which you are by yourself from the time you get up in the morning until you go to bed. If you can manage a full weekend or several days for this reflection, then do it.

I find that most Christians have never taken even a one-day private retreat. They resist the thought of spending so much time alone and setting other responsibilities aside in order to do it. My question is, can you afford *not* to do it? Next to your decision to follow Christ, you are facing the most important choice of your life in your decision about marriage.

You should choose a pleasant, reflective environment for this getaway. It should be away from normal distractions and a place where you will not expect to be interrupted. A regional, state or national park can provide an excellent and inexpensive setting, depending upon weather and seasonal factors. A hotel room, especially at a beach or vacation resort, can work well also. A superb alternative, if available in your area, is a Christian retreat center. Many conference centers which cater to groups also make provision for individual and silent retreats. Often the cost is less than a commercial hotel room.

What to Do on Your Personal Retreat

I recommend beginning your retreat time with some Scripture reading, to focus your mind on God's grace and sufficiency. Picking several psalms at random and reading them slowly and reflectively is an excellent idea. Follow this with a time of prayer. Spend a generous portion of that time thanking God for his past provision in your life.

Focus especially on relationships, particularly on the one you have come to pray about. Thank God for bringing the two of you together and for as many positive factors in the relationship as you can think of. Thank him for the challenges you've experienced in the relationship and for any other aspects of the relationship that come to mind. Thank him too for the confidence you can have about the future—the knowledge that he will protect you and guide you within a plan that reflects his very best for you.

Then pray that God will guide your decision about marriage and give you the mind of Christ in making it. Ask that he will give you the strength to do his will and to take the steps of faith involved. Ask him to give balance to your thinking—to keep you from being either unreasonably idealistic or too quick to compromise. Ask him to work out his very best in your life and your partner's.

Spend the remaining time reflecting on your relationship and its future, thinking through the possibility of marriage as thoroughly as you can. It may be helpful to take this book along and to reread part three in order to identify as clearly as possible the issues with which you need to be concerned. Carefully consider your relationship, noting the positive and negative factors. You may find it beneficial to write down your thoughts. Try listing in columns the pros and cons of going ahead with marriage. Then, reflecting on this list, consider which direction seems to be more appropriate.

As the day moves on, note carefully whether one impression about what to do seems to be stronger than the others. Do you lean toward marriage, away from it or toward waiting for further insight? Don't look for perfect certainty—a psychological impossibility for most of us—but for *substantial* assurance about which direction to take. If you feel reasonably assured that you should marry, I would take that impression as reliable at this point. This is the point where you are justified in taking a step of faith. Go ahead and resolve to marry. If perchance you've made the wrong choice, trust that God will make that clear to you in the days ahead.

If your assurance is not strong enough, then of course you shouldn't push yourself to a decision but should decide to wait for further insight. If you feel strongly that marriage is not recommended, then you should decide not to marry and be honest in sharing that with your partner. Pray that God will give you compassion and sensitivity as you share this conclusion with him or her.

Whatever your decision, close your personal retreat with another period of prayer, thanking God for his guidance during the time and requesting his continued direction in your relationship. Ask him to redirect any unjustified conclusions you have reached and to overrule any wrong decision you might have made.

Keeping Your Head

During such a time of personal reflection, you may experience a strong inspiration about what direction to take. It's very easy to think that this inspiration is a direct revelation from God, little short of an audible voice telling you what to do. But more often it's a psychological experience, not God revealing himself in a direct manner. You're discovering what it is underneath that you really want to do or think you ought to do. This insight is extremely important in understanding what God wills for you. If you have committed your meditation time to God and asked him to lead your thoughts, you can trust that the conclusion you've reached is guided by him. It is indicative of what he wants you to plan on doing at this time.

I choose my words carefully, for this is something short of saying that God has *directly revealed* to you what to do. If you think the latter, you'll be inclined to believe that God has laid an irreversible mandate on you to marry, giving you a revelation about the future. In reality your understanding of his will at this point is only as good as the information to which you've been exposed. It's possible that unexpected new information could suggest the need to change your decision. You at least need to stay open to this possibility, even after making a firm decision to marry, up until the time you finally take your vows.

I don't mean to imply that such a change will be likely. It's unlikely now that you will make some radically new discovery that will suggest revising your decision to marry. Yet none of us knows the future, and that possibility can never be discounted. Again we are thrown into the realm of walking by faith at each point of our journey toward marriage.

At the same time, even if you become firmly convinced during a personal retreat that you should marry, you will probably have some apprehensions between then and when you finally walk the aisle. Second thoughts will be normal. Unless there is some overriding and obvious reason why you should rethink your choice, though, you should hold firm to your decision to marry. If your mood swings are so great that you feel compelled to call off the engagement, and if there is no strong and clear reason for doing so, you should look carefully at whether an underlying fear of commitment is keeping you from being able to stay the course toward marriage. Read carefully the material in part five of this book. Again, though, remember that some fear and doubt in the face of a step as enormous as marriage is very normal.

Look for substantial certainty, not perfect assurance. Then go ahead in that confidence, even if some apprehensions recur.

Part Four

Should I Remarry —
or Marry Someone Divorced?

Fifteen

Remarriage

A Gift of God with Special Challenges

JEREMY, THIRTY-NINE, AND PRISCILLA, THIRTY-SIX, HAVE BEEN DATING seriously for over two years and would like to get engaged. They match up well at important points, and all of the lights seem green to get married. Except one.

Jeremy was married once before, to Angela, for ten years. Although she was the one who initiated the divorce, when he was thirty, Jeremy readily admits that his immaturity in the marriage contributed significantly to its breakup. Yet the divorce was a wake-up call to Jeremy to grow up, and he determined to meet the challenge. In the years since he has striven to strengthen his relationship with Christ, has attended a variety of divorce recovery workshops and has been active in a men's support group. For the past two years he has seen a counselor who has helped him greatly with his sensitive insights.

Both Jeremy's counselor and his pastor are convinced he is ready to marry again and will not repeat the mistakes that helped destroy his first marriage.

But Jeremy and Priscilla both wrestle with the biblical teaching on divorce and remarriage and wonder if Jeremy is free in God's sight to marry again. They want their marriage to be fully in God's will and not merely a second-best alternative.

Jeremy has been unsettled also by the emphasis in so much divorce recovery material he has read on the challenges and pitfalls of a second marriage. He wonders if he is truly ready to take the plunge and whether the tradeoffs are worth it.

Priscilla is unsettled by factors in their situation that are far from academic. Jeremy has partial custody of the two children from his first marriage, ages eleven and thirteen. Marrying him would mean becoming an instant parent, as well as needing to interact regularly with his ex-spouse and occasionally with her parents.

Priscilla struggles as well with another challenge—emotional, but still very real. She grew up thinking of divorced people as subhuman, incompetent creatures who had failed at life's most important endeavor. She determined that she would never marry a divorced man. Her friendships with Jeremy and several other divorced individuals have led her to shed her image of divorced people as losers. Still, it's hard to fully let go of old feelings, and she worries that she might be settling too easily by marrying him.

A Maze of Issues

It's difficult enough for most ordinary mortals to resolve a decision about marriage. When one or both of a couple are divorced, the agony can be beyond belief. My heart goes out to folks like Jeremy and Priscilla, for neither Christian nor secular culture makes the decision very easy for them.

There are many voices in the body of Christ telling those in Jeremy and Priscilla's situation that God, emphatically, does not permit them to get married. Many believe it is contrary to God's will for any divorced individual to remarry. Others are convinced he allows it only under certain conditions—usually if the divorced person's spouse had an affair or abandoned the marriage.

Those Jeremys and Priscillas who conclude that Scripture allows them to marry still face other discouraging influences. Divorce recovery literature sometimes stresses the challenges of remarriage over the benefits to a numbing extent; this is especially true of Christian material. As a result, many end up focusing more on potential problems than on the strength Christ would give them if they took a step of faith.

Then there is the divorcé-as-leper problem. Regardless of how one comes out on the issue of God's will and remarriage, many have trouble letting go of long-held biases about divorced people. Consciously or unconsciously these ingrained perceptions make it hard for someone like Priscilla to feel comfortable marrying a divorced individual, even when all of the other signals say go.

My personal conviction—and it's a strong one—is that many divorced people *should* remarry and *need* to remarry, and that many who have never been married will find their best possible match in someone who has been married before. Before you stone me (I realize this is a debatable point among the best Christian minds),[1] please at least hear my rationale. Hopefully we can stay friends, even if we agree to disagree.

Since the biblical issues are typically the greatest stumbling block for those considering marriage where divorce is involved, we'll look at them first in this chapter and the next. We'll then consider the practical and emotional challenges in chapter seventeen.

The Gospels' Hard Sayings
Many Christians conclude from studying Scripture that God categorically forbids divorce and remarriage in all cases. Others conclude that he permits them under certain limited conditions but forbids them in all others. Most who hold prohibitive positions on divorce and remarriage base them on Jesus' teachings in the Gospels. While the Old Testament law under Moses permitted divorce and remarriage, Jesus, in four passages in the Gospels, equates both divorce and remarriage with adultery (Mt 5:31-32; 19:3-12; Mk 10:2-12; Lk 16:18).

In Matthew 5:31-32, for instance, he declares, "It has been

said, 'Anyone who divorces his wife must give her a certificate of divorce.' But I tell you that anyone who divorces his wife, except for marital unfaithfulness, causes her to become an adulteress, and anyone who marries the divorced woman commits adultery."

Jesus does make an exception here to the rule that divorce and remarriage involve adultery—the case where one's spouse is guilty of "marital unfaithfulness," a point he repeats in Matthew 19:9. Scholars disagree, however, over what the term *porneia*, used in both of these statements for marital unfaithfulness, actually means. While some understand it as a synonym for adultery, others regard it as a more restricted term referring to unfaithfulness during the betrothal period or to incestuous marriage.[2] Because this word isn't employed elsewhere in the New Testament, it is difficult to determine for certain how Jesus understood it, and we may never know for sure.

Regardless of how we understand the exception, there is no question that Jesus meant to tie both divorce and remarriage in general with adultery.

Yet it is one thing to conclude this and another to say how Jesus meant it to apply to the real-life situation where one is *already* divorced, truly repentant for his or her role in the marriage breakup, and now facing an opportunity to remarry. Most who believe that Jesus' teaching rules out the possibility of remarriage have not adequately considered the *forgivability* of one's sins related to divorce. Even the best scholars who take a "no remarriage" position based on the Gospel passages usually have failed to wrestle sufficiently with the impact of Christ's atonement in this matter.

Consider that nowhere in the epistles do we find a statement clearly declaring that a divorced believer is forbidden to remarry. While Paul offers some appropriate cautions about remarriage in 1 Corinthians 7, as he does about marrying in general, he stops short of declaring unambiguously that one must never remarry. Nor does Jesus himself state things so specifically. When we consider how far-reaching the impact of a decision to remarry is, it is reasonable to expect God would have made any prohibition about remarriage in Scripture unmistakably clear. It would not have been left as a matter over which the best Christian minds have the potential to disagree.

What Jesus Said—and What He Didn't

What, then, was Jesus' purpose in making such severe statements against divorce and remarriage? He certainly meant to discourage divorce and to challenge popular permissive attitudes about it. He clearly meant to stress God's ideal that marriage is forever—the most binding commitment into which two people can enter. But he stopped well short of declaring that there is no forgiveness for those who fail in an attempt at marriage and never the possibility of a second chance.

There is another level on which Jesus made these statements. Jesus preached exacting moral standards at times, not to lay a compulsive lifestyle on people, but to point out how utterly impossible it is for one to live up to God's perfect moral code. He meant to sound a wake-up call, to help people understand how desperately they needed the forgiveness he would later offer—needed a savior who would gain them entrance into heaven. He meant to encourage *humility*, not an obsessive effort to live the godly life in one's own strength.

In the Sermon on the Mount, for instance, just before his statement about divorce and remarriage quoted above, he declares:

> If your right eye causes you to sin, gouge it out and throw it away. It is better for you to lose one part of your body than for your whole body to be thrown into hell. And if your right hand causes you to sin, cut it off and throw it away. It is better for you to lose one part of your body than for your whole body to go into hell. (Mt 5:29-30)

In spite of Jesus' clear admonition in this passage to cut off any portion of your body which makes you prone to sin, we have no indication—from all of the information we have about the

early church in Acts and the Epistles—that any responsible
Christian ever followed this practice. To the contrary, Paul chas-
tised those who taught abasement of the body as essential to salvation (Col 2:23). Paul did confess that the more completely he
understood his own vulnerability to sin, the more fully he appreciated his need for Christ's salvation (Rom 7). Jesus' teaching on
amputating one's hand or eye probably heightened Paul's appre-
ciation of his inability to please God through the law. It undoubtedly helped other Christians in the same way.

Yet the early Christians clearly understood Jesus' atonement
as adequate to forgive their sins completely, removing any requirement for mutilating their bodies because of sin. In this case
they regarded his atonement as covering their actual sins and
their *implications* as well.

In all likelihood they understood Jesus' teaching on divorce
and remarriage in this same spirit. It wasn't meant to lay a compulsive requirement on divorced persons: that they are forbidden
by God ever to remarry. Rather it was intended to bring home to
such persons how urgently they need Christ's forgiveness and
cleansing. And undoubtedly they understood his forgiveness as
not only covering the sins involved but erasing their implication
that remarrying would be committing adultery and violating
God's will.

Missing the New Testament's Bottom Line

At every point we are in danger of selling short the atonement of
Christ and of missing the full impact of what Paul meant when
he insisted, "There is now no condemnation for those who are in
Christ Jesus" (Rom 8:1). Many evangelical Christians regard divorce as an unpardonable sin in some respects, in a different category in terms of punishment and consequences from any other
sin.

Consider the irony: no one would claim that a never-married
woman who has engaged in fifty affairs but is now repentant is
forbidden by God to marry. The Christian community, in fact,

would encourage her to get married, regarding it as a positive step toward getting her life together and putting it on a firmer moral foundation. Nor would anyone suggest that God would deny a repentant serial killer the opportunity to marry. Yet many believe that a man or woman who has failed just once at making a marriage work is forever required by God to remain single. Do we really believe that the eternal God is this regimented and selective in how he looks upon human sin and metes out discipline?

From this angle, we should require extraordinary evidence before concluding that Scripture rules out remarriage for some or all divorced individuals. In fact, such unmistakable clarity simply isn't there. And when we realize how extensively Scripture understands Christ's atonement as forgiving *all* human sin, we should assume it fully covers the sins related to divorce—to the extent that a divorced person can become free before God to remarry.

Remarriage and Adultery

Some scholars who agree with this conclusion still insist that a couple commits adultery by marrying if either are divorced. God may will for them to marry, yet hold them guilty of adultery for taking the step. Those who hold this position, based on Jesus' statements in the Gospels,[3] usually assume the individuals are guilty of only a single act of adultery by marrying, that they may be forgiven and thereafter be considered legitimately married.

While I appreciate the effort of these scholars to reconcile Jesus' hard sayings on divorce and remarriage with his forgiveness, I still believe their position fails to give adequate credit to his atonement. And it paints God as mercurial—forgiving the divorced person's sins, even leading that person to remarry, then bringing those sins to mind again by regarding the act of remarriage as adultery. This view falls short of the radical promise of forgiveness God declares in Isaiah 43:25: "I, even I, am he who blots out your transgressions, for my own sake, and remembers your sins no more." Or the extravagant assurance of Psalm 103:12: "As far as the east is from the west, so far has he removed our transgressions from us."

Divorced persons who have fully faced their own culpability for the broken marriage and have genuinely sought Christ's forgiveness should rest assured they are in a clean-slate position before God to consider remarriage. And without taking a major step backward to take one forward. To conclude anything else is to devalue the atonement of Christ.

But what about Paul's teaching on divorce and remarriage in 1 Corinthians 7? Does it not draw boundaries around the possibility of remarriage that we haven't considered? In the next chapter we'll look at this question and the counsel Paul offers.

Sixteen

Paul's Balanced Counsel on Remarriage

CHAPTER 7 OF 1 CORINTHIANS IS THE ONE PLACE OUTSIDE OF THE Gospels where the New Testament presents significant teaching on divorce and remarriage. Paul's counsel in this chapter provides further encouragement for a divorced person to remarry under the right circumstances. Unfortunately, his teaching is sometimes taken to say just the opposite, because his style of language is misunderstood.

Paul declares in verses 10-15:

> To the married I give this command (not I, but the Lord): A wife must not separate from her husband. But if she does, she must remain unmarried or else be reconciled to her husband. And a husband must not divorce his wife.
>
> To the rest I say this (I, not the Lord): If any brother has a wife who is not a believer and she is willing to live with him, he must not divorce her. And if a woman has a husband who is not a believer and he is willing to live with her, she must not divorce him. . . .
>
> But if the unbeliever leaves, let him do so. A believing man or woman is not bound in such circumstances.

It is easy to read these passages and conclude that while Paul may allow separation or divorce under certain circumstances, he forbids any divorced person to remarry. Verse 11, for instance: "she must remain unmarried or else be reconciled to her husband."

It is critical, though, to understand Paul's style of speaking in these instances. Throughout 1 Corinthians 7 he is presenting not absolute standards but general principles for the Christian life which apply to many but not all believers. To say it better: he is giving default guidelines that should be our beginning point in decisions about singleness and marriage; we should base our choices on them unless we have strong evidence to do otherwise. Paul uses two approaches to convey that he is speaking generally and not absolutely: (1) referring to what is "good" and (2) employing the imperative form for many action verbs throughout this chapter, which is less emphatic and binding than other Greek verb forms.

Rules and Exceptions

Paul begins his discussion in 1 Corinthians 7 declaring, "It is good for a man not to marry" (v. 1), a theme to which he returns several times in the chapter. As the chapter unfolds it becomes clear that he doesn't mean staying single is good for all people or, in this case, even most, but for *many*, including himself. His point is that we shouldn't hastily choose to marry but should begin with the default assumption that God wants us to remain single unless the burden of proof suggests otherwise.

Paul quickly assures us that the burden of proof can be met. In verse 2 he states, "But since there is so much immorality, each man should have his own wife, and each woman her own husband." Now it sounds as if he is saying every person should marry! His point, though, is that we should marry if our sexual desire is so strong that we find it a burden to stay chaste as a single person. He clearly isn't giving an absolute command that we *must* marry; not every person can find a suitable partner, and Paul never implies one is sinning by not marrying. Rather, he uses the imperative verb form, which is best rendered, "let each man have his own wife, and let each woman have her own husband." He is giving a general principle, which we should follow if circumstances allow, but not a binding moral command.

Paul continues this same flavor of language when he speaks of remarriage. His counsel to the divorced woman in verse 11, which the NIV renders, "she must remain unmarried or else be reconciled to her husband," uses the imperative verb which is more accurately rendered, "let her remain unmarried." His style of speaking in the first part of his discussion on singleness and marriage suggests that he is now presenting a default guideline to the divorced person. She should remain single, and strive to reconcile with her spouse, unless the burden of proof strongly suggests otherwise. Paul surely means to discourage one from divorcing in order to marry someone else, as well as hasty remarriage after separation. One's default assumption should be that she should reconcile, and she should make an earnest effort to do so.

But Paul does not insist in any absolute way that she must remain forever unmarried, any more than he presents absolute requirements about staying single or marrying in verses 1-2.

Paul continues his use of the imperative verb in verses 12-15, quoted above. The NIV's "musts" in verses 12-13, for instance, are simply not there in the Greek, and Paul's counsel is more accurately rendered, "let him not divorce her," and "let her not divorce him." Paul is giving the rule to which one should make an earnest effort to comply. But he does not say there are never exceptions.

Further Evidence That God Allows Remarriage
Paul returns to the theme of divorce and remarriage in verses 27-28 of 1 Corinthians 7, declaring:

> Are you married? Do not seek a divorce. Are you unmarried? Do not look for a wife. But if you do marry, you have not sinned; and if a virgin marries, she has not sinned.

Vital to understanding Paul's intention in these two verses is that the term rendered "unmarried" in verse 27 in the NIV is more accurately translated "divorced." In the Greek it means literally "released from a wife," and uses the identical root verb employed in the expression the NIV renders "seek a divorce" in the previous sentence. The RSV much better captures Paul's thought in verse 27 by translating it, "Are you bound to a wife? Do not seek to be free. Are you free from a wife? Do not seek marriage."

Even better is the NEB's rendering, "Are you bound in marriage? Do not seek a dissolution. Has your marriage been dissolved? Do not seek a wife."

This distinction is a critical one, for when Paul states in the next verse that one does not sin by marrying, he is actually referring to a *divorced person's* marrying. Paul is saying literally that a man who has been previously released from a wife is not sinning by remarrying.

Paul is again speaking in the default mode in this passage, saying that as a rule a married person should not divorce, and a divorced person should not remarry. Yet by indicating that a divorced person does not sin by remarrying, he implies that there are exceptions to these rules. One should have strong evidence that a change is recommended, but this evidence is present in some cases.

Marriage as a Means of Grace

When Paul's broader intent in 1 Corinthians 7 is understood, I believe we have compelling evidence that divorced persons should feel free before Christ to remarry under the right circumstances. One of Paul's primary concerns in this chapter is to stress that God gives us marriage not because we deserve it but because we need it. An important purpose of marriage is to help us avoid immorality, by giving us opportunity to focus our sexual and romantic energy on one person. While Paul stresses that we should be certain we really need the benefits of marriage before going ahead, he stresses equally the importance of being open to marrying if our need is strong.

So we are brought to a critical question: What basis does anyone have for assuming that divorced persons need the benefits of marriage any less than never-married individuals? Far too often our Christian discussions about remarriage fail to consider the divorced person's *needs*. Yet if marriage is intended to be a means of grace, through which God helps us to avoid immorality and to focus our energy in a healthy manner, we should require extraordinary evidence that Scripture categorically rules it out for any group of people, including those who are divorced.

Again, we simply do not find such indisputable clarity on this point in Scripture. Indeed, when Paul speaks directly about marriage as a means of grace, his language is inclusive; he does not imply that any group of people should be denied marriage's benefits. Rather, he insists:

> Since there is so much immorality, each man should have his own wife, and each woman her own husband. The husband should fulfill his marital duty to his wife, and likewise the wife to her husband. (vv. 2-3)

> Now to the unmarried and the widows I say: It is good for them to stay unmarried, as I am. But if they cannot control themselves, they should marry, for it is better to marry than to burn with passion. (vv. 8-9)

> If anyone thinks he is acting improperly toward the virgin he is engaged to, and if she is getting along in years and he feels he ought to marry, he should do as he wants. He is not sinning. They should get married. (v. 36)

In these passages Paul declares that each person who needs marriage should seek it. He doesn't suggest, for instance, that it's acceptable for a divorced person to burn with passion by staying unmarried, but not for anyone else. His counsel seems inclusive, directed to anyone who truly has the need.

Paul's return to the point in verse 36 that one does not sin by marrying is also interesting. Here he draws no restriction to the rule that, if one's need is strong, he or she does not commit sin by marrying.

Does Paul suggest that it's possible for one to sin by *not* marrying? He never states matters this strongly. But he is clear that God provides special grace through marriage to help us face a world of immorality. Nowhere in Paul's writings or anywhere in Scripture do we find clear evidence that divorced persons are somehow in a "special exception" category where they should be denied this benefit.

In fact, when the total mix of factors is considered, we come to a quite different conclusion. A divorced person who continues to experience a strong need for marital companionship may reach the point where he or she should be *encouraged* to seek remarriage. If we insist they not do so, we may be guilty of requiring them to live the Christian life in their own strength, rather than in the grace Christ would provide through remarriage.

Seventeen

Meeting the Challenges, Beating the Stigmas

IN NOTING THAT SCRIPTURE GIVES DIVORCED PERSONS LIBERTY TO remarry, I do not mean to minimize the challenge of reaching the point where remarriage can be a life-giving option. Time is always needed to recover from the trauma of divorce and to grieve the marriage breakup. Even those who are relieved to be free from a bad marriage still need significant time to come to terms with lost expectations and to adjust to their loss.

Most who have suffered a divorce need to do plenty of self-examination and soul-searching. Even one who hasn't been primarily responsible for the divorce still needs to come to grips with how he or she may have contributed to the marriage's failing. Does the divorce signify problems in their behavior that are likely to sabotage a future marriage? Does it indicate that their process of choosing a mate is flawed?

Most important, how can the person avoid these tendencies in the future? What are the steps they need to take to grow—to learn to face life contentedly now as a single person and to reach the point where marrying again is a healthy alternative?

The help of a competent counselor in sorting these things through is usually indispensable. Divorce recovery workshops, such as those offered by Fresh Start Ministries, are often invaluable.

Most counselors and pastors agree that a divorced person should allow at least two years for healing and growth before taking the step of marriage again. Many need longer recovery periods.

You Can Do It

With all of this in mind, my heart goes out to many divorced people who, far more than needing admonitions and proper cautions, need encouragement to get back onto the horse from which they've been thrown. Divorce recovery teaching and literature sometimes dwell on the potential pitfalls of remarriage to an almost dizzying extent. You can be left feeling that the mountain you must climb to be ready is so high that you can't possibly breathe at that altitude.

I fully agree that the challenges of the second marriage usually exceed those of the first, sometimes considerably so. Yet you are older and, hopefully, wiser at this point. You may be fully ready to take on these challenges. And they may be exactly what will keep you in the best state of dependence upon Christ.

As I never tire of stressing, God gives us marriage about equally for our fulfillment and for our development. Within the arena of marriage he not only extends encouragement to us but stretches us in countless beneficial ways. Through relating to our spouse, our spouse's friends and extended family, and the children who come into our life, God teaches us to love others who are different from ourselves. He deepens our compassion for people and helps us to love others more readily and naturally. He increases our ability to handle many other challenges of life as well.

A second marriage brings unique challenges. Yet given where we are in our personal development, the overall impact of these challenges may not be any greater than those of a first marriage. It *is* vital that we weigh the challenges carefully. And it's essential that we know ourselves well enough to judge soundly if we are able to handle the demands of marrying again. Yet it's just as important that we be willing to take a courageous step of faith with our life. Those who are divorced may need more than the usual amount of encouragement to go forward, even when the time is clearly right.

Marrying a Divorced Person: The Important Issues

I feel sad as well for those like Priscilla who have a good opportunity to marry someone divorced yet feel unreasonable hesitations. Even if they are persuaded Scripture allows them to do so, the step of marriage still presents them with significant challenges—some real, some imagined. They will find it enormously helpful to identify these challenges and think clearly about them. When those in Priscilla's position carefully weigh them, they often find that these are occasions to which they can rise.

These challenges can be boiled down to three:

☐ *Weighing the cost.* Marrying someone who is divorced often means assuming responsibilities you wouldn't have if he or she hadn't been married before. You may be inheriting children from your spouse's former marriage, full- or part-time. If so, then you will probably have to relate on some level to your partner's former spouse, to that person's parents, and possibly to other friends and relatives of the ex as well.

Your partner may have an ongoing financial commitment to the ex-spouse or to children; you will always have to take these expenses into account in planning your family budget.

Yet these are challenges that can be met. And countless people navigate these waters quite well, convinced the tradeoffs are worth it for all that they gain through the marriage. The important matter is to know yourself. Are you are at a point where you are ready to take on these challenges? Do friends whose judgment you trust agree? Is there a pastor or counselor who is persuaded this is the right step for you?

If so, then go for it. Look upon the challenges as an opportunity for growth, and focus upon the joyful aspects of the marriage. Don't be dissuaded by all the pessimistic voices you hear stressing the potential problems. Your situation is unique, with certain challenges and rewards that no other marriage has. Keep your head. Look clearly at the genuine challenges you'll face, and weigh carefully whether you're ready to tackle them. But don't invent problems that aren't there.

Most of all, focus on Christ and draw on his strength. Trust that as you stay close to him, he'll give you the grace needed daily for the adventure ahead.

☐ *Weighing the risk.* It's equally important to determine if your partner is ready for remarriage. Is it likely that he or she will stay faithful to you? Are you confident this person will not repeat the same patterns that contributed to the failure of the previous marriage?

Here are the most crucial issues to consider:

1. Has reasonable time elapsed since the previous marriage broke up and the divorce was final? You have particular reason to be cautious if it has been less than two years.

2. Does your partner talk openly and humbly about his role in the marriage breakup? Has he clearly faced his own culpability for what happened? Beware especially if humility is lacking, or if he blames his ex-spouse for everything that went wrong.

3. Has she made a concerted effort to grow at points where she hurt the former marriage? Has she sought counseling, attended divorce workshops or support groups? Do friends who know her well feel she has turned the corner at necessary points and is ready to marry again? Is there at least one competent professional who knows her well and can give you an objective opinion?

4. Are you confident he wants to marry you for healthy reasons? Does he treasure you for your unique qualities and not for how you compare in some way to his former spouse? See a red flag if he views you as strongly similar to his ex or as her diametrical opposite. Again, it is a good idea to get the opinions of those who know him well.

Each of these issues deserves careful scrutiny. If there are any to which you cannot give a reasonable yes, you should not go ahead with marriage right now. At the least, you should allow the other person more time to heal and grow.

Yet I stress *reasonable* yes, for this person you care so much about falls well short of perfect, and if you expect perfection at any point you'll drive yourself crazy looking for it. Nor should you expect perfect certainty about the future. With all the messages you hear about the risks involved in remarriage, it's easy to end up expecting a level of assurance that just isn't reasonable.

You simply cannot remove the element of risk, no matter who it is you are marrying. Looking for substantial certainty is important—but perfect certainty isn't attainable. At some point you have to be willing to take a reasonable risk and go ahead with marriage.

Here's something especially encouraging to consider. It can be a better risk to marry a divorced person who has profited from his past mistakes than someone who has never been married before. We are comfortable with this concept in every other area of life. How often we hear it said that someone has succeeded in business, or in sports, for instance, because she first failed, then learned from her failure how to do things better. This same dynamic can apply to remarriage, and often does. Yet we seldom hear this point emphasized, due, I'm certain, to our uneasiness in general with divorce. It is hard for us to imagine that something positive might emerge from it.

☐ *Dealing with stigmas.* Which brings us to our final concern. Even if you are comfortable biblically with marrying a divorced person and confident your partner is a good choice, you may still feel uneasy about going ahead. Your hesitation may result from commitment anxiety that you would experience in marrying anyone. Yet it may spring also from negative stereotypes about marrying someone divorced—stereotypes that you have carried in the past and have never fully shed.

We idealize marriage in American society to a degree that is outlandish in terms of the real-life choices every one of us faces. We each have our check list for the perfect mate, and on it are criteria that are not reasonable in light of how God made us and his best intentions for our life. You may have grown up vowing never to marry someone divorced, or only as a last resort—a second-best option. Perhaps you've revised that viewpoint, even radically, yet the impact of that old attitude still nags you. Or you may have a conscious conviction that marrying a divorced person is settling for less than the perfect ideal.

It helps to remember that God's best for us in any area—his very, very best—often appears to us to be less than perfect, especially at first. There is no area where this is more true than in choosing someone to marry. It seems to be the rule, not the exception, that God's best appears to us as a diamond in the rough.

When we realize that God's purpose in marriage isn't only to bless us but develop us, it begins to make sense that he would not want our partner to perfectly meet our ideals at every point. If someone did, that person would become an idol to us. Our affection for them would be anything but healthy, and our well-being would depend far too much upon how well the relationship was doing.

I have seen many wonderful marriages take place where one or both of the people have been married before. I'm convinced some of us will find our best possible match in such an arrangement.

The way to deal with any stigma like this is to face it honestly, own it, do what you can to overcome it—but above all, don't let it control your decision making. Think of your choice to marry as *a step of faith*. Move out in spite of fears, in spite of doubts, and even though all of your ideals aren't fully met. I'm not speaking of blind faith, where you throw all caution to the winds. You should have substantial reasons for making your choice. But it's just as important to consciously act against unreasonable hesitations that are holding you back. Knowing it's not only okay to do so, but necessary, makes it easier.

Stigmas are overcome more by acting than by analyzing. By taking action you open yourself to experiences that put the lie to your stigma and help you more fully to let go of it.

If you have a good opportunity to marry someone who is divorced, assume in faith that this is God's best and not second-best opportunity for you. Greater confidence will follow as you move forward.

Part Five

Confronting the Fear
of Commitment

Eighteen

Understanding the Fear of Commitment

"I'M ENGAGED TO BE MARRIED NEXT AUGUST, AND RECENTLY I'VE BE-come so scared of the event. I love this man with all my heart, and I'm certain he will make a terrific husband, but I am terri-fied. I cry about it often, and it truly scares me. I grew up in a nearly perfect home, and part of me is afraid to leave that. An-other part of me is afraid that I won't be able to follow in their footsteps of perfection. I have some days of joy when I think of the wedding, and other days I panic. What should I do? I truly love this man, and I feel guilty and ashamed of having these thoughts."

That is how a woman recently described to me her apprehen-sions about marrying. Her testimony is similar to countless oth-ers I've received in letters, e-mails and personal conversations since publishing the first edition of this book.

While the fear of rejection keeps many from moving toward marriage, others are hindered by a quite different apprehen-sion—the fear that they might be too successful. They dread the thought of being locked into a binding relationship, with all the responsibility, trappings and loss of freedom involved. It's the fear of commitment that holds them back.

Often those who fear commitment do long for the benefits of

an intimate relationship. Yet the thought of losing freedom so frightens them that they experience conflict within and may display erratic behavior. An approach-avoidance pattern results; it appears bizarre to anyone who doesn't understand the nature of the fear. Such persons move toward intimacy at one point in a relationship, away from it at another.

Normal Jitters

Some apprehension in the face of a step as momentous as marriage is not only normal but healthy. If you don't feel at least some fear, you have neither appreciated the element of risk involved nor weighed the cost carefully enough. No matter how carefully the decision is approached, any thinking person realizes that a decision which will radically affect the rest of life is being made on the basis of very little information. No decision forces you to confront more fully the frailty and limits of your own thinking.

There is, too, a normal process of grieving as you face up to the loss of personal freedom involved in getting married. No matter how greatly you long to be married, there is sacrifice involved. While the tradeoff in a good marriage is always much more than worth it, still there is grief over what you are giving up to become permanently attached.

When Marjorie agreed to marry Ted, she was strongly confident she had made the right decision. But as their wedding day approached she became increasingly anxious. What if she was making the wrong choice? What if Ted turned out to be a different sort of husband than she imagined? What if she found marriage to be too confining?

Wisely, Marjorie sought advice from a counselor. After reviewing her reasons for deciding to marry Ted, the counselor assured Marjorie that she had made an excellent choice. He told her, too, that her fears were quite normal and understandable and that she would be wisest not to let them hinder her from going ahead with the wedding.

Marjorie left the session relieved. Up till this point she had assumed that when God leads a person to marry, no doubts or fears intrude. Now at least she was no longer afraid of her fear, for she realized she wasn't abnormal for having some apprehension. Though she continued to feel some jitters up to the day of the wedding, she went ahead with it and afterward felt immense relief. It was clear now that she had to take this step simply to put her fears to rest. She and Ted have been married for nine years now, and she has never wavered in her confidence that she took the right step.

The type of doubts and apprehensions which Marjorie experienced during her engagement period are the rule and not the exception for those who take a mature approach to marriage. They are part of the adjustment process involved in making the momentous leap from singleness to a lifetime commitment. Most people, when they come to understand how normal it is to have these fears, are able to deal with them, rise above them and move on to marriage. And most, like Marjorie, find that once the vows have been taken, their fears vanish. Until that point there was always the opportunity to change their mind, and knowing that made them prone to reanalyzing their decision. Now, with the final bridge burned, they are able to feel a degree of confidence they hadn't known before.

Don't Fence Me In

For some, though, the fear of commitment takes on a more serious dimension. For them it is nothing short of a phobia. When the fear of commitment reaches this level, it truly interferes with their ability to do what they most desire or believe is best. It is not enough for them simply to be told it is normal to be fearful, or to be assured of Christ's protection, for their level of discomfort is so great they can think only about getting immediate relief from it.

The fear of flying is a common phobia experienced by about 20 percent of Americans. It is similar to the fear of commitment in many ways. No amount of consoling statistics or exhortation to trust the Lord frees the white-knuckled flyer from his dread of flying or his sense of entrapment once aboard an aircraft. The fear is an irrational, disabling one resulting from many learned emotional and physical responses that cannot be undone in a moment.

For one who is phobic about commitment, the dynamics of the fear are much the same, only the object of fear is different. This person may greatly enjoy dreaming about the possibility of marriage (just as the fearful flyer indulges pleasant fantasies about flying when a trip is not impending). And this person may strongly desire the benefits of marriage (just as the phobic flyer wants the extensive advantages of travel which flying provides). Yet when faced with the imminent reality of commitment, this person panics and feels the same claustrophobic entrapment that phobic flyers experience once the cabin doors slam shut.

Though it may sound overdramatized, for some the fear of commitment is every bit this severe. Like all phobias, the fear of commitment comes in varying degrees. For some it is strongly debilitating, for others only mildly so. I find it most helpful to think in terms of four levels at which the fear of commitment commonly occurs.

Level One: The Screeching Halt

Eric courted Judy relentlessly for five months, getting only indecisive replies. Finally, as they were driving home from a singles retreat, Judy said that she had had time that weekend to think it over and that, yes, she would like to be his wife. Eric was so overjoyed that he nearly drove the car off the road.

Yet the next day Eric seemed unusually cold and distant when he phoned Judy at her office. He explained that an emergency had come up at work, and he would have to work late the next several evenings. Each time they spoke on the phone that week Eric seemed jittery and anxious to get off as quickly as possible. Though perplexed, Judy wrote it off as work stress.

Then the bombshell. When Judy arrived home Thursday evening, a note from Eric was taped to her apartment door. It read, in part, "I've come to realize that I made a big mistake in thinking we should get married. The Lord has shown me this week that it isn't his will for us to be together and may not be his will for me ever to be married at all. The reasons are deeply personal and have nothing to do with you at all. I'm really sorry, as I know I got your expectations up. Yet I know nothing will be gained by talking about this. Let's just trust this to the Lord and move on."

All attempts to contact Eric in the weeks that followed were either unsuccessful (he made himself as unavailable as possible) or unproductive (he was cold and refused to talk about their relationship). Finally, mortified and bewildered, Judy gave up, assuming she must have made some terrible mistake which turned Eric against her.

Though Eric's behavior following Judy's acceptance of his offer of marriage seems incomprehensible, it is a more common response than many realize.[1] His discomfort rose to such a level that he could think only of escaping. Judy was left shaking her head, wondering what she possibly had done to provoke him. In reality, Eric left not because the relationship was bad but because it was good! Nothing Judy could have done—short of refusing his proposal—would have prevented him from walking away.

Often persons with extreme commitment fear desire the benefits of an intimate relationship as long as the pressure of a binding commitment is not there. Frequently, too, they imagine that they really do want a permanent relationship. Usually it is security needs that trick them into such a deluded mindset. They need to know their partner will commit to them for the sake of their own self-esteem.

Yet once they know that the other will commit—and expects them to be committed—they panic. Because their fear of being locked into a relationship is greater than their desire for a relationship, they want out. When this fear reaches the level that Eric experienced, they can think only of breaking free as quickly and completely as possible. This accounts for (but of course does not excuse) the brutal and insensitive way in which commitment-phobic persons sometimes break things off. Their anxiety runs so high that they cannot think of the other's needs but only of their own need to break free.

Level Two: On-Again, Off-Again

Another level of commitment fear, while less extreme than Eric's, is still quite debilitating. It is epitomized by the on-again, off-again response.

During the two and a half years that Andy and Melissa dated, Melissa agreed no less than five times to marry him, including two formal engagements. Within one to seven days following each of these acceptances, she was plagued with severe doubts and, with great embarrassment, told Andy she couldn't go through with marriage at that time. Yet never did she want to break up with him. Each time she begged him to give her more time to sort through her feelings and make a decision. And in time she always came back to a point of conviction and told Andy with considerable confidence that she would marry him. But within a short period the doubts intruded again, and Melissa broke things off.

Though a remarkably patient person, Andy finally reached his limits and broke up with Melissa. Yet during the year since, Melissa has continued to intimate that she would like to get back together with him and is open to discussing marriage. Andy continues to wonder if he is being too harsh and if it's reasonable to expect that in time Melissa will actually walk the aisle with him.

As with Eric, Melissa's fear of commitment is greater even than her desire for a marriage relationship. Yet it is not so great that she feels compelled to flee the relationship altogether when commitment panic sets in. Rather, she takes steps to keep the relationship intact while freeing herself of any immediate obligation to the future.

Once the immediate pressure of commitment is off, she begins to feel comfortable in the relationship again. In this state she begins to dream again of the advantages of marriage and starts to imagine that she can overcome her fears just by trying a little harder. Given the right inspirational setting—a Sunday-afternoon canoe ride or a candlelight dinner—she warms to the idea of marriage to the point of wanting to commit, and she does so with confidence. Then her fears take over and the pattern repeats.

Level Three: Ongoing Ambivalence

For some the fear of commitment is about equal to their desire for marriage. Sam's relationship with Rebecca demonstrates this well. They have dated over three years. They have talked often about marriage and have spent long hours dreaming together about what it would be like to have a family, a home and a life dedicated to one another.

Rebecca has been quite up-front in telling Sam that she would like to be his wife. Sam has told Rebecca that he loves her more than anyone he has known, that he knows she would make a fantastic wife and that he cannot imagine being married to anyone but her. Yet Sam, an impressively honest man, has consistently added that the thought of a binding, forever-type commitment frightens him. At the same time, he has pleaded with Rebecca to be patient and to give him time to grow out of his fears. He doesn't want to lose the prospect of marrying her.

Rebecca, who also cannot imagine being married to anyone other than Sam, has continued to cherish the hope that he will eventually come around. Yet after three years, her patience is wearing thin, and she wonders if she's wishing for the moon. Though Sam has remained faithful to her, there hasn't been any clear evidence that he will ever change.

Because Sam's fear of commitment is not as extreme as Eric's or Melissa's, he is less prone to repress it and thus less prone to erratic behavior. In other words, because he is more aware of his fear and more up-front in dealing with it, he is less likely to make a commitment which he can't keep in the first place.

Yet Sam demonstrates a pattern which is common at this level of commitment fear: long-term inertia in a serious relationship. The relationship stays serious, with much talk and loving dreams about the possibility of marriage, but it always stays just a possibility. The moment of decision is never reached. Sam loves Rebecca and longs eventually to marry her. Yet *eventually* is the key to his attitude, for if it gets any closer, he freezes. He is like the person with a moderate fear of flying who longs to visit family members in a distant city and dreams often about it but can never take the final step to purchase a ticket and make the flight.

Relationships like Sam and Rebecca's sometimes go on for years, until the fearful one finally overcomes his or her inhibitions enough to break the inertia and make a commitment, or the other person finally gives up and bails out. There is greater hope that the persons at this level of fear can on their own eventually get beyond their inhibitions and make a meaningful commitment than there is for those at the first two levels. Yet it often requires an extreme measure of patience, understanding and sensitivity on the other's part, which, understandably, some are unable or unwilling to provide.

Level Four: Normal Apprehension

Finally, as we've said, there is a level where commitment fear can actually be termed normal—even healthy and nonthreatening—provided it is properly understood. At this point one's desire for marriage and intimacy is greater than one's fear of commitment. Yet, as we noted in Marjorie's case, some fear persists, due to humility about the limits of one's own knowledge and the process involved in letting go of old attachments to take on a new and more greatly desired one. Such fear, in right proportion, indicates that you are taking the decision seriously and working through the necessary adjustments involved.

The danger is that you may overreact to being anxious. This will especially be true if you assume that unbending confidence must always accompany any decision led by Christ. In that case you'll be inclined to take your uneasiness as a red flag to the decision to get married.

Like Marjorie, when most people are helped to put their apprehensions in right perspective, they are able to accept them and get beyond them. These hesitations don't end up being the hindering force that fears of a more phobic nature tend to be. To the contrary, apprehension at this level is actually a benefit, for it moves the person to depend on Christ and to appreciate the marriage decision more fully as the step of faith which it always must be.

Nineteen

· · · · · · · · · · ·

When the Problem
Is Your Partner's

HOW CAN YOU KNOW IF THE ONE YOU'RE DATING (OR THINKING OF dating) is fearful of commitment? Is there a way to spot this pattern before it becomes a problem in your relationship?

Your partner may be frank in admitting to you that he or she is apprehensive about commitment. Yet until you know someone very well, you cannot count on that person's being completely honest about areas that might jeopardize their chances in the relationship. Also, it is the nature of this fear, particularly at the more extreme levels, that it tends to get repressed, especially when one is not immediately faced with the prospect of commitment. Your partner may not recognize the existence of the problem, or may think that a past episode of it was an aberration from his or her true character. Yet unless this person shows clear evidence of change, you shouldn't assume that a past demonstration of commitment fear was an aberration. The chances are high that the pattern will occur again.

Looking at your partner's past history in relationships will give you important clues about his or her attitude toward commitment. You have a right to be suspicious if your partner has
☐ Abruptly broken off a relationship in the past shortly after committing to marriage.

☐ Demonstrated an on-again, off-again pattern in a past relationship.

☐ Broken off two or more relationships at some point after committing to marriage.

☐ Been involved in three or more serious relationships which extended for two years or more without being able to resolve whether to marry. (I'm speaking here not of situations in which someone else broke up with your partner or was the one who couldn't decide about marriage but of those in which your partner was the ambivalent one.)

To be sure, it's possible that your partner's past behavior resulted not from commitment fear but from an unrealistic perspective on God's guidance. He or she may have been expecting an unreasonable sign from God to confirm the marriage decision or may have been waiting for an impossible measure of inner certainty. It's also possible that your partner was harboring unreasonable ideals about a romantic relationship. This person may have modified his or her expectations and be in a better position now for a healthy relationship. If either of these is true, and if your partner has had a genuine change of perspective, then you shouldn't hold past behavior against him or her. This person deserves another chance.

But if there is no clear evidence that your partner's behavior resulted from problems of perspective, you can assume that this person is fearful of commitment. If your relationship reaches the commitment stage, the chances are strong that the pattern will repeat.

Keeping the Windows Closed

You should be *highly* suspicious if your partner is overly secretive about his or her life. It's common that those with extreme commitment fear will keep important windows of their life closed to those whom they date. One reason is the fear of getting too intimate with anyone. Another is the fear that the one whom they're dating will find out too much about their past relationships. In addition, they may be concerned to keep their escape routes open. The less their partner knows about the particulars of their life, the easier it is to disappear.

To be more specific, you have good reason to be uncomfortable with anyone who after several dates

☐ doesn't want to introduce you to their parents

☐ doesn't want you to visit their home

☐ is uncomfortable with your ever visiting them at work, phoning them at work or knowing much about the particulars of their work

☐ introduces you to none or few of their friends

☐ wants only to be alone with you, consistently avoiding any opportunity to be together with you in the company of their friends or business associates

☐ doesn't reveal specifics about trips they make—or gives dishonest or misleading details about them

Taking Control

Of course, determining that someone is fearful of commitment and deciding what to do about it are two different matters. If you are comfortable with the thought of having a serious relationship that may not end in marriage, then, of course, you are justified for staying in the relationship—only guard your heart.

If you are one who likes to court risk, you may want to try your hand at helping this person get beyond his or her commitment fears. Perhaps you have the gifts and disposition needed to help this person toward healing.

It is not terribly likely though, that someone at a level one or two commitment fear will be healed without professional help. You must accept the fact that your most important role may amount to convincing this person to get the professional counseling needed. Remember, too, that in the midst of your optimism you must keep your feelings in check; your partner may never be able to commit to you. You must be prepared for any outcome.

You are also quite justified in breaking off a relationship with someone who is fearful of commitment, just as you are justified in avoiding the relationship in the first place. This is not being uncompassionate (assuming that you handle things sensitively) but is simply part of being a good steward of your life. Remember that Christ has told us that we are to be not only gentle as doves but wise as serpents in our dealings with people (Mt 10:16). This principle must apply as much to the realm of romantic relationships as any other.

Too Close for (Your Partner's) Comfort

But what if your relationship is already at a serious stage and your partner has displayed one of the patterns I've described? First, let me say something about a level one response. If (heaven forbid) someone has abruptly broken off a relationship with you shortly after agreeing to marry, has been insensitive, distant or untalkative since and seems to have undergone a personality change, you can be fairly sure that he or she is commitment-phobic.

You are probably at your wit's end right now wondering what you did wrong or what you can possibly do to repair this tragic breach. It is vital that you understand that the relationship aborted not because of what was wrong but because of what was right. Your partner suffers from a severe fear of commitment, and it is very unlikely you will be able to change that. Though it seems very cold to say this, you will do best to abandon hope that this relationship will ever work out—and move on.

Most important, do not blame yourself for what happened. Learn what you can from this dreadful experience, and keep your guard up against it happening again. But remember that most people are not this severely phobic about commitment. Don't harden yourself against the possibility of trying again with a more stable person.

It sometimes happens that a person who abruptly and insensitively breaks off a relationship after committing to marry comes back weeks or months later and asks for another chance. With the threat of commitment now removed, what once attracted that person to you is now attracting them again. They may plead with you to give them another opportunity and may insist (yes, even with tears) that they will not treat you as they did before. It may be very tempting to give in.

Remember, however, that even though on the conscious level this person may be quite sincere, he or she has already demonstrated a serious lack of self-understanding in committing and then abandoning you before. What evidence is there that this person's self-understanding is any better now? You should only agree to a renewed relationship if he or she has either undergone a successful program of counseling to deal with the fear of commitment or is clearly willing to do so. Even then, you should guard your heart carefully until you have proof that your partner has actually grown in his or her ability to handle commitment.

Perhaps, though, you're in a relationship with someone whose fear of commitment is more of the level two type. If your partner has made a commitment to marry you and retracted it two or more times, yet still wishes to stay in the relationship, you need to look carefully at the reasons for this pattern. As we've noted, an on-again, off-again pattern can result from an unrealistic perspective on guidance (expecting unreasonable confirmation from God) or from holding onto unreasonable ideals. If, however, there is not some clear point of perspective that accounts for the erratic responses, or if your partner is not able to revise his or her perspective, again I must be a wet blanket and say that you are in a difficult situation as far as the prospect of marriage is concerned.

If you have the patience of Job, can tolerate your partner's inconsistency and are gifted at dealing with people psychologically—and if you are able to accept the possibility of not marrying this person—then you may be safe in maintaining the relationship. With this level of commitment fear, however, your partner more than likely will need professional help to get beyond it.

But what about a level three situation—that is, the long-term relationship that never reaches the commitment stage, even though both express much interest in marriage? This is the situation of commitment fear that I encounter most frequently among older singles. Here I'm comfortable giving you a rule of thumb for determining whether in fact level three commitment fear is present. If you both are into your mid-twenties or beyond, your relationship is well into the second year or beyond, and one wants to marry but the other can't decide—even though he or she strongly desires to maintain the relationship at a serious level—then it is probable that this person has at least a moderate fear of commitment. Again, the exception would be if there is some clear issue that is keeping him or her from being able to decide. If the issue is addressed, yet they still cannot resolve to marry, commitment fear is probably the cause.

Here you must make a judgment call, and you are frankly justified either for staying in the relationship or not. It is possible that if you bear with this person, your patience, sensitivity and tenacity will in time be used by the Lord to help them over the hump of indecisiveness. You must steel yourself for the possibility that this will never happen. Yet because this person's fear of commitment is about equal to their desire for marriage, there is a reasonable possibility that desire will eventually prevail over fear. It is also possible that this person can be persuaded to get professional help. Someone at this level of commitment fear is more likely to be open to it than those at levels one and two.

Getting Outside Help

Be aware that the same fear that makes your partner apprehensive about committing to marriage may cause him or her to be uneasy about the commitment and intimacy involved in regular counseling sessions. Though he may promise earnestly to seek help, don't be surprised if there is no follow-through. It may take the most extraordinary gentle persuasion skills you can muster to get your partner off dead center on this one, especially if this

174 Should I Get Married?

person's level of commitment anxiety is high.

If you have resolved that you will stay in the relationship only if your partner faithfully seeks help, then you should set the following minimum guidelines:

1. He or she should seek out a pastor, psychologist, psychiatrist or professional counselor who is skilled in treating phobias and who understands the dynamics of commitment fear. While it is always nice if the counselor is a Christian, it is not absolutely necessary if he or she is at least respectful of your spiritual stance. Because the need is for healing from a specific fear, not the broader concern of gaining perspective on life itself, you do best to get help from someone who understands the dynamics of phobias. (In the same way I wouldn't hesitate to recommend that you go to a non-Christian surgeon for removal of a ruptured appendix, if that person was the best one available to perform the operation.)

Finding the right person may take some shopping around. You can begin by asking your pastor for references, but don't hesitate either to ask for recommendations from your physician or local hospital. If you are not certain about the ability of a given counselor to help you, interview him or her with your partner and ask clear questions about that person's experience with this type of problem. In the end you will have to make a judgment call about the capacity of each counselor to meet this need. Move on till you find one in whom you have confidence.

2. Once you have found a qualified counselor, it will be important for both you and your partner to meet initially with him or her, together or in separate meetings, to get a clear perspective on what course of therapy to follow. The counselor will probably suggest that your partner agree to an approximate number of sessions (perhaps ten). It will be important for you to know this and to be aware of whether your partner is actually following through with them.

3. When the process is complete, you should meet with the counselor by yourself and get a clear evaluation as to your part-

ner's progress. If your partner objects that all of this amounts to your breathing down their neck too much, or if your partner tries to skimp on some of the details, you can conclude that they are not as serious about overcoming the fear of commitment as they need to be to justify your staying in the relationship. When the fear of commitment is at level two or above, authentic healing will require bold moves on both your part and your partner's. It is understandable if you don't want to get involved to this extent. But you should not count on miracles happening apart from counseling if you partner's commitment fear is high, any more than you should expect someone with a physical disease to get better without professional help.

Yes, the Lord can intervene and heal directly, and he does. He can do it with phobias as well as with physical problems. But you shouldn't be the one left with the burden of having to determine whether healing has really occurred. If your partner has been erratic in commitment in the past, the burden should be on that person to demonstrate conclusively that he or she is beyond putting you through this torture again. It is not asking too much that someone with professional counseling skill help in determining this and, if necessary, assist with the healing process.

In the next chapter I talk more directly to the person who fears commitment. I offer some guidelines to this person for determining whether to seek counseling, and encouragement to do so. I also suggest steps they can take on their own—with or without counseling—to overcome commitment fear. Encourage your partner to read that chapter. You may find it beneficial to read it as well, for further insight into how to help your partner and whether to insist that he or she seek professional help.

Twenty

....

When the Problem
Is Your Own

BUT WHAT IF FEARING COMMITMENT IS MY OWN PROBLEM? HOW can I take steps to deal with it?

Perhaps you already knew that you are fearful of commitment, or perhaps you've begun to suspect so as you've read the discussion so far. If you're not certain whether you are, let me advise you simply to look at your past history in relationships.

Have you had a relationship in which you desired marriage but then lost interest once the other became willing? Now that the relationship is over, do you look back with some regret and feel that in a sense you sabotaged a good situation? Have you been in a relationship in which you've fallen into an on-again, off-again interest in marriage—wanting it, but then getting frightened and backing off each time a commitment was made? Have you been in a long-term relationship in which you wanted to marry and the other was clearly willing, yet you could never bring yourself to make a final decision? Have you had several relationships that follow one or more of these patterns?

Again, it is possible that your ambivalence sprang more from problems of perspective than from fear. You may have been expecting God to tell you in some dramatic way that you have found the right person, or you may have been cherishing unreasonable ideals about what that person should be like. Perhaps the discussion in this book has helped you work through to a more healthy perspective and you are in a position now to move into a stable relationship.

Yet if there seems to be no clear point of perspective at fault here, the chances are strong that you are suffering from some unhealthy commitment fear. This presents you with a good-news, bad-news proposition. The good news is that, emphatically, you can overcome this problem. Your fears do not have to keep you from doing what underneath you dearly want to do.

The bad news is that emotional struggles are seldom overcome in a moment, through a single resolution of the will or stroke of miraculous healing. It takes persistent effort to gain the upper hand.

Yet with commitment fear the effort is much more than worth it, and it will likely benefit you in many areas beyond your marriage decision. And once you understand what is involved, you may decide that the road to healing is not so intimidating after all.

Take heart, too, that the fears you're experiencing, as debilitating as they may seem, do not signal that you are mentally ill or a neurotic freak. Your experience is extremely common, far more typical than Christians usually recognize. Commitment fear is at heart a phobia, and phobias, fortunately, can be conquered.

I'll address in a moment the question of whether you ought to seek counseling. But first let's look at steps you can take with or without professional help. Here are five areas where you should focus.

1. Increase your desire for marriage. Phobias succeed in derailing our most earnestly set goals for a simple reason—the intensity of our fear exceeds the intensity of our desire. The first step we need to take in seeking to overcome any unreasonable fear is to do what we can to turn up the velocity of our desire.

Doing this by itself sometimes makes a radical difference. As you think over your own life, you can probably remember many occasions when you were frightened to do something but found the resolve to do it as your desire increased. As our desire grows more intense than our fear, we find the courage to move ahead in spite of our fear.

Unfortunately, you are unlikely to pick up a book for Christian singles or hear a talk which is designed to stoke your desire for marriage. Christian writing and teaching almost universally urge singles not to be overeager for marriage. While this may be a redemptive theme for younger singles with multiple options, who need to take time to grow before jumping into marriage, it can be salt in the wound for older singles who are caught in the inertia of commitment fear. These individuals need to be encouraged to appreciate the benefits of marriage and to cherish them enough to move beyond their fears.

So I want to urge you to make more of an effort to focus on these benefits. For you they may include

☐ having someone constantly available with whom you can share your most intimate struggles and joys

☐ having someone who helps you resolve your most critical life decisions

☐ having a close companion as you enter older age

☐ enjoying the ecstasy of sexual relationships (without guilt!)

☐ having children, parenting and enjoying the multitude of extended relationships that result as your children grow older

☐ having an entrée to couples' activities

☐ material benefits and, with your spouse's help, better management of your finances

☐ developing a home where you can better entertain and minister to others

☐ having someone who challenges you to grow and who, even through their rough edges, is used by God to help you learn to better love and relate to other people

☐ and last but not least, having the marriage decision resolved once and for all (so you no longer have to agonize over whether to get married)

Make a list of the benefits of marriage that are most important to you. Review this list each evening before you go to bed and first thing when you wake up in the morning. Verbalize your list—read it aloud. Carry it with you, and review it several times during the day, when you have free moments.

You may benefit as well from taking a personal retreat to nurture your desire for marriage. Plan a day or two in a quiet, pleasant setting, where you do nothing but focus on the advantages of being married. Dwell on the aspects that are most attractive to you. Use this time to get more in touch with that part of you that longs to be married.

2. Increase your fear of missing the opportunity to marry and the benefits of marriage. While many people are overly anxious about missing the chance to marry, those who fear commitment often are not anxious enough. Some legitimate fear of the consequences of taking the easy way out is always part of finding the courage to take any difficult step.

Remember that life is not infinite, and choices do not present themselves forever. Regardless how long-suffering your partner is with your ambivalence about marrying, patience may not last forever. The point may come, and sooner than you think, when he or she decides to let go of this tortuous relationship and move on.

While it's important to dwell on the benefits of getting married, it's just as important to appreciate that you may miss them by not taking action—even to feel anxiety about that. Consider that by not going through with your present opportunity to marry, you may be turning your back on the chance of a lifetime.

If you desire to parent children, it is essential to respect your biological clock. I'm speaking to both men *and* women here. While women who want to bear their own children often have a profound sense by their mid-thirties that time is running out, men find it easier to punch the snooze alarm on their biological clock. Yet if you are male, keep in mind that you are better able to keep up with the demands of parenting small children in your twenties and thirties than as you approach mid-life. Both of you, in fact, should keep in mind not only the woman's physical capacity for bearing children but your energy level for parenting as well.

The insidious result of commitment fear is that it can keep you from doing what you genuinely want to do. Staring into the abyss of what will happen if you cave in to this fear is an important step toward breaking its grip.

3. Let go of unreasonable ideals. Unreasonable perfectionism in thinking toward marriage, as we've noted, can be a problem by itself and does not necessarily signal commitment fear. Yet most who fear commitment have overly perfectionist standards for whom they will marry.

Examine your own outlook carefully. If you have begun reading this book with this section on commitment fear, you may benefit by going back and reading earlier portions, especially part three on judging compatibility. If you find that, in all honesty, you are too idealistic in your standards for a spouse, work at modifying your expectations. Focus on your partner's positive features, and learn to laugh at the more human ones. Remember that it's not only *okay* to marry someone who fails to meet all of your ideals but *necessary* in order to enter a good marriage. God provides us with a suitable partner but not a perfect one.

It can be a great relief to realize you don't have to saddle yourself with finding someone who perfectly matches all of your ideals. Enjoy the freedom that comes from being more flexible.

4. Let go of unreasonable concern for guidance. It is equally important not to be rigid in your expectations of guidance from God (another problem that can exist apart from commitment fear but often accompanies it). Desiring to do God's will is important. But don't expect God to give you some special sign that you should marry this person apart from the logical understanding that this individual is a good match for you. In the vast majority of our decisions God guides us not through dramatic means but by directing our thinking, even though we may not feel as if we're being guided. God doesn't normally absolve us of responsibility for making our choices, even in a decision as momentous as marriage. Aim for reasonable certainty in your choice—but not perfect certainty.

It may help you to read part two of this book on guidance if you haven't already. *Knowing God's Will* is a book that also tackles this topic in depth.

5. *Manage your panic reactions.* Often the most debilitating aspect of commitment fear is a panic reaction that you don't fully understand. You only know that it sets in whenever the prospect of marriage or engagement gets too close for comfort. Many who suffer from commitment anxiety have told me of the most severe phobic reactions associated with it—including sleeplessness, inability to eat well and heart palpitations.

Fortunately, there is much you can do to manage panic reactions, regardless of their cause, and even defuse them altogether. It takes practice, but it can be done. Because the emotion of fear is so closely connected to physical reactions, altering these responses can diminish the feeling of fear significantly. Mental discipline helps as well, particularly making a determined effort to halt obsessive thinking the moment it starts. Here are some steps that are commonly recognized by phobia therapists as effective in combating the onset of fear.[2]

☐ *Practice abdominal breathing.* When we're stressed, our need for oxygen increases. Typically we breathe more intensively but into our chests. This "thoracic" breathing results in part from our esteem for the military posture—"stomach in, chest out!" Yet in this position our lungs are not able to expand to receive their full capacity of air. The result is that we feel the need to breathe more quickly, and hyperventilation may occur. When under stress, we need to counter our natural tendency toward chest breathing. Let your stomach relax (and hang out if necessary!), then breathe slowly and deeply into it. Hold your breath for several seconds, then slowly let it out. The tranquilizing effect is remarkable. Continue doing this until your sense of control returns.

☐ *Relax muscles you tend to tense.* The next time you feel panic coming on, make a point of noticing your muscular responses. Do you clench your hands? Cross your legs tightly? Fold your arms? Tighten your stomach muscles? Push your toes together? Many of us who, like myself, have a frontal bite, clench our teeth. All these reactions increase our stress levels. The clenched jaw, in fact, can produce a number of other unfortunate side effects, including dizziness, distortion in the ear, migraines and facial pain.

Learn to identify your muscular reactions under stress, then make a conscious effort to counter your natural inclinations. Practice relaxing your muscles when you feel tense. Open your hands and let them hang loosely. Let your jaw hang limp. Resist the temptation to cross your legs or clamp them together. When relaxing the muscles is combined with proper breathing, the physical effects of stress and panic are greatly reduced. We can experience a considerably greater measure of control over our anxiety responses when these practices are followed.

☐ *Follow a healthy routine of rest, eating and exercise, and general management of your time.* We need to take sensible steps to eat properly, get the rest and exercise we need, and manage our time carefully. In general, anything which contributes to our physical well-being helps to reduce our general stress level. Like many people, my appetite diminishes when I'm anxious or fearful. I find, though, that when I neglect my normal eating habits my vulnerability to being anxious increases. If I'm feeling nervous about a trip or a talk, I think of eating as an act of discipline (at other times it's a wonderful celebration, but not now). I make myself eat a normal meal, even though I'm not particularly eager to do so. Again and again I find the simple step of keeping food in my stomach reduces stress.

☐ *Practice thought-stopping.* Finally, we need to take a bold step of mental discipline to thwart obsessive thinking. Specialists who work with phobia sufferers recommend the practice of "thought-stopping."

When an unreasonable fear comes to mind, immediately yell

internally (or externally, if no one is around), *Stop!* It may help to picture a policeman holding up a large stop sign, blowing his whistle incessantly and commanding you to halt. Be absolutely consistent in doing this every time an irrational thought troubles you. Insist that it cease and desist. Then immediately replace the fearful thought with a pleasant one. Think of a situation that you find relaxing or encouraging. Remind yourself, too, of God's absolute care for you, his desire for your very best, his forgiveness, and his complete acceptance of your feelings.

The important thing is being consistent and persistent in this response. Over time, when combined with other practices I'm suggesting, thought-stopping helps significantly to change patterns of phobic thinking.

These steps will help you greatly in reducing crippling anxiety about commitment and other phobic reactions as well. If you are serious about conquering chronic commitment fear, recognize that your learned emotional reactions are part of the problem. You have developed a *habit* of fearing commitment. Fortunately, habits can be broken. You never have to be the victim of runaway emotions.

God has given us much greater ability to defuse the emotion of fear than we normally realize. We are even capable of reversing our instinctive responses to phobic situations.

Should I Get Professional Help?

A major question remains, and that is whether you should seek professional counseling for help in overcoming commitment fear. There is fortunately far less stigma attached to doing so than just twenty or thirty years ago. Still, you may feel squeamish, especially if you have never talked with a counselor before.

Let me remind you that commitment fear is keeping you from doing what you *want* to do. I urge you to love yourself enough to be willing to do whatever it will take to conquer the problem. Counseling can make a radical difference in helping you gain control. And you will likely find that the process is far less unsettling than you imagine; chances are good you will find that you enjoy much of it. With a good counselor you are able to share about your most intimate struggles without being judged, and you receive constructive advice that goes beyond what any book or lecture can provide, for it touches on the unique particulars of your life.

In deciding whether counseling is the right step for you, consider these four factors:

1. The severity of your fear. As best as you can, rate the intensity of your commitment fear. Use the four levels we spoke of in chapter eighteen, realizing that your fear may fall somewhere between them.

In weighing the severity of your fear, consider especially your behavior in relationships. Have you ever bailed out of a relationship shortly after committing to marry? More than once? Have you displayed an on-again, off-again pattern in your present relationship or in previous ones? Do either of these patterns seem *habitual* for you? If so, then your fear is almost certainly at level one or two.

In this case I cannot urge you strongly enough to seek professional counseling. What these patterns signify is that you repress your fears, and probably other feelings as well. You do not understand yourself well. A competent counselor will help you identify your feelings better and make healthy responses to them. This understanding will be invaluable to you in all areas of your life, and it will make the time and expense involved with counseling very worthwhile. And it may make all the difference in your being able to move beyond the control of your fears into an enduring commitment to marry.

2. Your family background. None of us comes from a perfect family. Yet if your upbringing was highly unaffirming or abusive, then chances are good you have been wired to fear success in relationships. You may feel guilty about attaining a quality of relationship that your parents never enjoyed. And because you were deprived of it during your childhood, committed love is outside of your comfort zone. While you long for it on one level, when it's within your grasp it seems unspectacular; you are more instinctively attracted to relationships that are unavailable to you.

A good counselor can help you probe your background, identify the factors that cause you to sabotage good relationships, and learn to make healthy choices that override your mood swings.

3. *Your personal capability for trouble-shooting your own psychological issues.* Some of us are more naturally gifted than others at thinking psychologically and understanding our psychological makeup. How successful have you been in the past at identifying the causes of emotional struggles and overcoming them? Most us benefit from outside help when an emotional problem seriously upsets our life.

4. *Your partner's needs.* Even if you're not convinced you need outside help, consider the statement you're making to your partner. If you're in a relationship where you've demonstrated commitment fear, then you've lost credibility with him or her. Especially if you've made a commitment to marry but then retracted it, your partner may find it hard now to trust you that you'll follow through in any effort to deal with commitment fear.

By agreeing to see a counselor you're demonstrating to your partner that you're taking an aggressive step to deal with the problem. You're also bringing accountability into the picture. This may be precisely what will cause your partner to feel right about giving you more time to grow comfortable with commitment.

Strongly weigh your partner's needs as well as your own in deciding whether to seek professional counseling.

Be Decisive

Let me stress something that is perhaps obvious. The fact that you fear commitment in relationships means you may be uneasy with the commitment required in counseling as well. Turn the tables on your psyche here. Taking a decisive step to commit to sessions with a counselor, and keeping that commitment, will in itself be therapeutic. It will have positive ripple effects in all other areas of your life, helping you grow more comfortable with commitment in general.

If you know or suspect that you need the assistance of a counselor, take the challenge. Some guidelines for locating a suitable counselor are listed at the end of chapter nineteen. Review them, find a counselor who is appropriate for your needs, and commit to the meetings he or she recommends. You will experience many rewards for rising to this occasion.

For further reading, I have written a full book on conquering the fear of commitment, *The Yes Anxiety.* You will find help on our Nehemiah Ministries web site as well (www.nehemiahministries.com).

Dealing with Normal Apprehension

Finally, as we've stressed, some fear is normal in taking a step as major as marriage. Some fear is actually healthy, for it gives you over to the reverent attitude needed for entering a lifetime commitment. It is healthy *if* it doesn't paralyze you or cause you to walk away from a good opportunity for marriage. If you have made a commitment to marry, or are on the verge of doing so, and are experiencing fears of the manageable type, you probably don't need professional help in dealing with them (though it certainly won't hurt to seek encouragement from a pastor or counselor). What you most need is assurance that you're not abnormal for having these fears and that they don't by definition mean that you've missed the leading of God in your decision.

You may also find it helpful to take a short personal retreat. Get away by yourself to a pleasant, reflective setting for a day or so. Thoroughly review your reasons for marrying this person. If, in this meditative environment, you feel confident about your choice, then go ahead and don't let normal nervousness dissuade you.

Put your trust in the absolute sufficiency of Christ to protect you and even redirect you, if perchance you have made the wrong choice. Then determine to put your hand to the plow and not look back.

Remember, too, that most of our anxiety about the future results from worrying about how we might cope with given problems. Scripture promises, though, that God will give us exactly the grace we need to deal with each contingency of life. While this principle underlines all of Scripture, it is stated most expressly in my favorite verse of the Bible: "And from his fulness have we all received, grace upon grace" (Jn 1:16 RSV). The Greek literally states "grace following grace," implying a continual flow of grace, or more specifically, fresh grace every split second of our existence! Yet it is characteristic of grace that it's never given until the very moment we need it. Our anxiety results from trying to predict exactly how God will give grace for a problem. But we can never know this until the moment comes. We can only know that when it arrives, the grace will be there. This is why Jesus urged us to live each day unto itself (Mt 6:34).

This perspective on grace is perhaps the most important thought you can keep in mind as you move toward marriage, with the multitude of uncertainties ahead of you. Most of the problems you worry about will not occur. Yet if they do, God's grace will be more than sufficient for your moment of need.

Christ intends the Christian life to be an adventure. Our greatest happiness and our greatest fruitfulness come when there is a reasonable measure of adventure in our life. Frankly, our modern evangelical teaching stresses the security part of Christianity too much, whereas Scripture lays much more emphasis on the adventure involved in walking by faith. While God does meet important security needs through marriage, I'm certain that the adventure side of marriage is even more important in God's design of human life. Once we accept that adventure is *supposed* to be involved in a step of faith, that step becomes easier to take and the challenges seem less intimidating.

If the thought of moving toward marriage frightens you, think of it as an unparalleled opportunity for adventure.

Dwell on that thought.

And dwell on the protection and grace which Christ promises to provide you.

With those assurances in mind, go ahead.

Take the plunge.

And may God be with you and uphold you each step of the way.

Appendix One

....

To Date or Not to Date

THERE HAVE ALWAYS BEEN CHURCHES AND MINISTRIES WHICH HAVE discouraged or forbidden dating and provided members with alternative means for finding someone to marry. Interest in non-dating approaches to finding a spouse became mainstream in the late 1990s with the publication of two books: *I Kissed Dating Goodbye* by Joshua Harris and *Choosing God's Best* by Don Raunikar.[1]

Harris and Raunikar both argue that dating is such a highly flawed process that one who is serious about finding God's best for marriage should forgo it altogether. Instead, trust that God, who is the ultimate matchmaker, will find a way to guide you to the person you should marry without the need for dating. He will likely use friends, family and church associates to help you find this person. You should be strongly convinced this person is God's choice before agreeing to an intimate relationship with him or her; once this relationship is initiated, it should be regarded as no-turning-back—a betrothal that should end only in marriage.

Harris, who was only twenty-one when he wrote his book, presents his philosophy with considerable humor and self-deprecation. He admits some will not agree with him and that the non-dating approach may not be the perfect answer for everyone.

Raunikar, on the other hand, is more emphatic in declaring that dating is by its nature such a temptation pit that one cannot possibly honor God by engaging in it. As an alternative he proposes "courtship," through which you get to know someone in casual and group situations well enough to determine if they are God's choice. You declare to each other you are convinced you should marry, then move immediately to engagement, which Raunikar argues should usually be brief.

My primary concern in *Should I Get Married?* isn't with dating and the process of finding someone to marry but with making a good judgment about whether to marry someone who is available to you. This book is for those already in a serious relationship or considering one—to help them understand God's guidance, weigh their compatibility, and move beyond unreasonable fears. The principles I recommend should apply regardless of the process you follow in finding a mate—whether you seek to do so through dating or a nondating approach.

I need to address the dating issue at least briefly, though, for the process we follow in seeking someone to marry invariably affects how we decide whether to marry that person. If the process I choose allows me to get to know the person well, I'll be able to make a well-informed choice about marrying them; otherwise, I may be forced to rely on hunches or unusual guidance from God.

If I want to be married yet opt not to date, I need to be clear about how I expect to make a responsible decision about marrying someone. Do I have a dependable means for getting to know others of the opposite sex well outside of dating? Are there others whom I can rely on to help me find and identify someone suitable? And is it reasonable to think I can find someone who will be open to considering me for marriage without going through the normal process of dating?

Too often the answers to these questions are no. This is my major concern with the don't-date philosophy. In most social settings in America today it is highly difficult to get to know someone well enough without dating to be in a position to decide responsibly about marriage. Most people do not have others who are qualified and prepared to help them in the process. One is thus inclined to look for unreasonable guidance from God that someone is his choice before initiating a serious relationship. One becomes susceptible to the spiritualizing of God's will and the expectation of advance certainty that we've counseled against, with all the problems that can result. If I commit to marry someone on the basis of such "guidance," I'm left with little wiggle room if I discover once I know this person better that we're not well-matched for marriage.

A related problem is that most singles in our society are not in a good position to meet someone willing to consider marrying them without going through the dating process. Indeed, their stance against dating may scare potential candidates away.

Traditional Matchmaking Worked Well

It shouldn't have to be this way. Dating has been a popular social practice for less than a hundred years, and in only a limited portion of the world. Throughout most of history most people have found their spouses without the aid of dating as we now know it. Traditional approaches to finding a spouse are still common in many countries today and enjoy broad social support.

Yet where matchmaking without dating has prevailed throughout history, it has been anything but an irresponsible process. Typically, the whole society has been geared up for it. Parents, relatives and friends of the young man or woman seeking a mate have helped that person find someone suitable, and skillful professional matchmakers have often been employed. Where the person being matched has been passive, others have been very active and taken care to find someone compatible with that person's family background, temperament, goals and expectations. While faith has often played an important role in traditional matchmaking, there has been plenty of human initiative involved as well.

A Revealing Example in Scripture

We don't have to look beyond Scripture for an excellent example of traditional matchmaking, carried out responsibly with key social support: Abraham's effort to find a wife for his son Isaac.

Abraham faced no little challenge in finding someone right for Isaac. Not only did the young woman need to be from his own blood line but spiritually and personally compatible with Isaac as well. That ruled out the women of the Canaanite community where they now lived.

So Abraham did the logical thing. He decided to look in his former home region of Haran. Since he was too old and infirm to make the journey himself, he delegated the role to a trusted servant.

When we think of this most beloved of romantic episodes in the Bible, we tend to remember how Abraham's servant sought God's guidance through prayer and was dramatically led to Rebekah. The story, which spans the longest chapter in Genesis (chap. 24), profoundly underscores the role of prayer and faith in this remarkable sojourn.

Yet it speaks just as strongly to the responsible initiative that was part of the process of finding Rebekah. And bold initiative at that. Abraham refused to be limited by his geographical confines but went beyond them. And his servant displayed considerable courage in being straightforward with Rebekah and her family about his mission. Rebekah could have rebuffed him. And if her family didn't believe him, it could have meant his life.

The story brings out how the whole social structure of Isaac's time worked to help him and Rebekah find each other. Abraham focused strongly on his son's need to find a wife. His servant and helpers played a critical role. Just as important were the expectations of Rebekah, Laban and their family. As soon as they heard of the opportunity available for Rebekah to marry Isaac, they were willing to let her do just that—unequivocally. They did not expect that Isaac first needed to prove himself *personally* to Rebekah.

It is this social climate of expectations and personal initiative that has been at the heart of effective matchmaking in countless societies throughout history. And it explains why matchmaking without dating has worked so well.

The Reality in North America Today

It also explains why it is not likely to work so well in North American society today. While societies past and present have provided a socially supportive environment for matchmaking apart from one's own initiative, such a climate simply doesn't exist in most sectors of our society in the twenty-first century. Most people grow up expecting to take considerable personal initiative to find their mate and not counting on others to do the work for them. It is incumbent on us to make for ourselves a responsible choice that in generations past would have been made for us. Most people expect dating to be part of the process of getting to know someone well enough to decide responsibly about marrying them.

If you expect God to provide you a mate without your going through this process that most in our society consider normal, you may be pushed beyond the boundaries of healthy faith into presumption—even into tempting God. It may be naive to think you can get to know someone well enough in this social climate apart from dating to make a sound decision about marriage to them. It may be equally presumptuous to expect that someone else would be willing to marry you without being courted through this expected social practice.

An exception would be if you're a member of a sector of society that supports a nondating approach to matchmaking and provides a reliable, responsible means for you to meet someone compatible. This is the case with Joshua Harris, author of *I Kissed Dating Goodbye*. The church to which Harris belongs, Covenant Life in Gaithersburg, Maryland, encourages members not to date. Elders and others in the church take active initiative to help singles find someone compatible to marry. It is also a large congregation in a sprawling suburb of Washington, D.C., with a sizable singles population. Because the social climate supports matchmaking without dating, activities—planned and spontaneous—often arise where men and women can get to know each other apart from the private route of dating.

For a single to commit herself to the hope of finding someone suitable to marry at Covenant Life Church without dating may be a responsible act of faith. Especially so if she agrees with the church's theological tradition, is active in singles events and makes a reasonable effort to let others know of her interest in marrying.

Rudy's Dilemma

How different is the case of Rudy, a resident of West Bend, Indiana. As a thirty-two-year-old Christian single, Rudy strongly desires to be married but is tired of the dating scene. He has read Harris's and Raunikar's books and likes their philosophies. He is seriously considering abandoning dating altogether and, as an act of faith, trusting God to bring the ideal partner to him without it.

Yet Rudy isn't aware of any church in his region with a large singles group that encourages and supports a nondating approach to matchmaking. Prospects of meeting someone compatible at his own small church seem nil: a new single hasn't joined in over a year, and efforts to start a singles ministry have never gotten off the ground. Because of his family's long association with the church, Rudy feels committed to stay there. He also enjoys an effective ministry at this church teaching elementary Sunday school.

At a company picnic several months ago Rudy met Catie, who works in a different division of the large corporation that employs him. As they chatted, they found that they both had become Christians through the same campus ministry at the University of Indiana. This point of contact has left Rudy comfortable sitting with Catie at lunch when he runs into her at the company cafeteria. It has happened only three times, though, as their lunch schedules usually don't mesh.

Rudy is impressed with Catie and would like to get to know her better. He senses she is attracted to him as well. She is the one woman he has met in the last several years to whom he can imagine himself married. Yet he realizes he needs to know her much better before concluding for certain he should marry her, and of course she needs an equal opportunity to get to know him. He wonders if there is a way to get from A to Z without dating.

Unfortunately, Rudy doesn't know any of Catie's friends well, and he doesn't feel comfortable approaching them cold to ask them for information about her. Rudy doesn't have friends who would be willing or able to go to bat for him on this either. There is no obvious way for them to get to know each other well apart from agreeing to spend time together.

Rudy is considering phoning Catie and explaining his situation to her. He'll tell her he is attracted to her and wants to know if they could commit themselves to consider each other as potential partners for marriage. He'll explain that he has forsaken dating (and why) but would be open to any nondating activities that would give them a chance to deepen their relationship. Can they rearrange their schedules to have lunch more frequently in the cafeteria? Can they plan to spend significant time talking on the phone and e-mailing? Does Catie have any other suggestions?

Rudy has read Catie correctly on several things. She is attracted to him, and she would be open to considering him for marriage. She would indeed make an excellent partner for him, as he would for her. Yet Catie is a product of her culture. She has long expected that the right man for her would woo her through dating. She also would consider it pretentious for Rudy—or any man—to talk seriously about marriage before they had been on at least a handful of dates. She has never heard of the concept of two mature Christians committing themselves to consider marriage without dating.

The Catch-22 is that if Rudy tries to explain the nondating concept to Catie, it will be too big a jump for her, given that their relationship isn't more developed. Since she doesn't know Rudy well, she will worry that his uneasiness with dating reflects unhealthy traits—laziness, tightness with his money or time, or fears of commitment.

No Perfect Process for Matchmaking
Those who advocate a nondating approach to finding a mate would insist that Rudy should simply trust the Lord to change Catie's heart. If God truly wants Rudy and Catie to marry, he will make it possible without dating being a part of the process. A major reason Rudy needs to take this step of faith, it's argued, is that dating is too morally perilous an activity for the Christian. The enforced privacy and expectations inevitably tempt you into premature intimacy and sexual involvement.

While dating does pose unique perils, I don't agree that it has to be a bottomless pit of temptation for the Christian. I know literally hundreds of Christians in good marriages who got there through the route of dating. Many did so without compromising their standards. And many carry positive memories of past dating experiences as important points of personal growth (another argument of advocates of not dating is that dating often leaves you scarred with guilt and tormented memories).

The truth is that any process which brings people together presents its own inherent problems and temptations. The courtship process which Harris, Raunikar and others recommend as an alternative to dating is not at all exempt; I know people who have been badly hurt through it and unhappy marriages that have resulted from it. The major fallacy of the don't-date philosophy is its assumption that by changing the process of how people meet and court for marriage, sin and bad judgment can be eliminated or greatly reduced. It simply doesn't work that way. Sin is a product of the human heart much more than of any activity within which we operate, and it will find a way to express itself within any activity of life.

Just as we must determine to marry someone less than perfect, and as we must settle for many imperfect circumstances if we are to find a good marriage, we must get there through an imperfect process. There are no perfect processes for matchmaking or any human endeavor.

Dating can be done with integrity. Christians who determine to do so can navigate the challenging waters of dating without compromising their values and without being damaged for life. And they can through this process find someone suitable for them to marry.

I don't believe it is reasonable for Rudy to assume that God will bring Catie to him as a marriage partner apart from his courting her through dating. Not that God cannot do so if he wishes. But for Rudy to *expect* God to do it is not greatly different from his expecting God to provide him a new job without his going through the normal interview process and social protocols that are part of being courted for that position. We realize immediately that stewardship of our life demands that we follow social expectations in job hunting; it should be no less so in finding someone to marry.

Respecting Our Social Setting

Singles in America today are much more often in situations like Rudy's than Harris's. As much as they might like to find someone to marry without the necessity of dating, they simply don't have an adequate support system in place to do so. Even if they can put together such a network, it will work only if the person in whom they are interested understands the philosophy of not dating and agrees with it. Like Catie, that person may be too acclimated to the custom of dating to let go of it and may suspect anyone who wants to bypass it of having a hidden agenda.

For one like Rudy to expect God to provide him a spouse without dating is not reasonable, unless he places himself in a social setting where that expectation is widely shared by others.

Let me hasten to say that I am grateful for the effort of Harris and others to reform the process of courtship in our society. Any steps that can be taken to make the process less painful and less open to selfish manipulation are greatly merited. But the effort should be directed especially at those who are in a position to do something about it—pastors and Christian leaders. Pastors, for instance, ought to be challenged to make matchmaking a responsibility of their church—to set up a network of people who help singles find someone suitable to marry and to encourage the congregation to be open to nondating approaches to courtship.

Unfortunately, the effort to this point has been directed primarily not to those in leadership but to individual singles—counseling them to forsake dating and to trust God to provide them a spouse by other means. Instead, these people ought to be encouraged to find a mate through the process that is customary to the social setting where they find themselves. If they can change their social setting to a better one, fine, but if they feel compelled to stay in it, they need to live within its realities. If dating is an ingrained custom in it, they shouldn't be counseled to forsake it but to do it with the highest standards of compassion and moral integrity.

When Paul declared that he had "become all things to all people" (1 Cor 9:22), he set forth a principle critical not just to missionary and evangelistic work but to every area of life. The point is that in striving to accomplish any goal we should make a reasonable effort to accommodate ourselves to the customs and expectations of the people with whom we're involved. Doing so is a matter of proper stewardship of our life—of blooming where we're planted, of playing responsibly the hand we've been dealt. To expect God to give us success apart from making this effort is not healthy faith but presumption.

This need to accommodate ourselves to others' traditions should apply no less in finding a spouse than in other areas. If dating is the major courtship custom among the people with whom we live or socialize, then we should assume (again, apart from a compelling reason) that we will find God's best through participating in it. Here, as in most areas of life, the time-worn principle applies: "When in Rome . . ."

Appendix Two

....

Vows for the
Imperfect Marriage

WE LEARN EARLY THAT BEAUTIFUL PRINCESSES ARE SWEPT UP BY handsome knights and live happily ever after. Nothing is said about the human quirks and failings that are standard equipment for every human being. If we grow up hoping for a fairy-tale marriage, disappointment lies ahead.

It will be important for the two of you to talk together, before you marry, about the expectations each of you has for the other—and about the fears you each may have about yourself, that you will not be able to be a perfect spouse. When you acknowledge that imperfections are a part of life, it will take a lot of pressure off your marriage. You'll work hard to have a mutually satisfying relationship, but you won't carry guilt and shame around when difficult moments come along.

Here are some "vows" that may help your discussion. You may simply want to read them together as you face the fact that no two human beings will be able to live out a *perfect* marriage. Or you could create a little ceremony—private or with a few close friends—where you pledge to accept each other in spite of imperfections. You could even include in your wedding a few words that emphasize accepting each other as imperfect individuals. You are welcome to use the following statements verbatim, modify them, or let them inspire you to write your own "vows for the imperfect marriage."

Recite individually to each other (memorize or read):

I want you to be a perfect wife [husband]. I hereby pledge that I am ready to give up that unrealistic expectation. You are a wonderful person, but no human being is perfect. I will do my best not to require that of you.

Likewise, I am far from perfect. I ask that you be patient with my humanness. In return, I will try to listen, to cooperate, to forgive and ask forgiveness, so that our relationship can be open and mutually nourishing.

Then recite or read aloud together:

Jesus promised an abundant and joyful life to the very fallen and flawed people of his day. Together, in dependence on him, we pledge to seek that abundant life—a life of good communication, honesty, laughs and deep joy as we walk through the years together.

We recognize that God has given us marriage as much for our development as for our fulfillment, as much to strengthen our faith as to deepen our joy. We look to God to give us grace to love each other through both the pleasures and the challenges of our marriage. Through it all, may he increase our ability to love others with the love of Christ.

Notes

Chapter 1: The Search for Perspective
[1]M. Blaine Smith, *Overcoming Shyness* (Downers Grove, Ill.: InterVarsity Press, 1993).
[2]M. Blaine Smith, *The Yes Anxiety: Taming the Fear of Commitment in Relationships, Career, Spiritual Life and Daily Decisions* (Downers Grove, Ill.: InterVarsity Press, 1995)

Chapter 2: Does God Want Me to Be Married or Single?
[1]Rhena Taylor, *Single and Whole* (Downers Grove, Ill.: InterVarsity Press, 1984), pp. 6-7.
[2]Such as Paul's exuberant view of marriage in Ephesians 5:21-33. The relationship of husband and wife is compared to nothing less than that of Christ and the church.
[3]C. Peter Wagner, *Your Spiritual Gifts Can Help Your Church Grow* (Ventura, Calif.: Regal, 1979), p. 63.
[4]Herbert J. Miles, *Singles, Sex and Marriage* (Waco, Tex.: Word, 1983), pp. 147-50.

Chapter 3: Does God Have One Ideal Choice for Me?
[1]By Donna Walters and used by permission.
[2]I realize that the phrase in this verse, translated by the RSV as "to take a wife for himself," is rendered in two other ways by other translations: "to gain mastery over his body" (NEB) and "to guard his member" (NAB). I am following the conclusion of O. Larry Yarbrough, who devoted a major portion of his Ph.D. thesis to examining 1 Thessalonians 4:3-8, that the RSV translation is the most reliable one. See O. Larry Yarbrough, *Not Like the Gentiles: Marriage Rules in the Letters of Paul* (Atlanta, Ga.: Scholars Press, 1985), especially pp. 68-76.

Chapter 4: How Can I Know God's Will?
[1]See my book *Knowing God's Will: Finding Guidance for Personal Decisions* (Downers Grove, Ill.: InterVarsity Press, 1991), especially chapter fourteen, "Inward Guidance" (pp. 165-72). See also my *Yes Anxiety*, chapter eight, "Guidance and Intuition" (pp. 91-98).
[2]Nita Tucker with Debra Feinstein, *Beyond Cinderella: How to Find and Marry the Man You Want* (New York: St. Martin's Press, 1987), p. 57.
[3]Again, see my *Knowing God's Will* for a full chapter on this issue (chapter thirteen, "Putting Out a Fleece" [pp. 156-64]). See also my *Nehemiah Notes* article "Fooled by Fleecing," available on our website at <www.nehemiahministries.com/fleecing.htm>.
[4]For those who wish to do a more in-depth biblical study of this issue, in appendix one of *Knowing God's Will* I examine exegetical issues related to authority relationships for parents, spiritual leaders and spouses (pp. 219-27).
[5]Michael Harper, *Prophecy: A Gift for the Body of Christ* (Plainfield, N.J.: Logos, 1970), pp. 26-27.

Chapter 5: Can I Be Certain?
[1]Charlie W. Shedd, *How to Know If You're Really in Love—Really in Love Enough for Marriage* (Kansas City, Mo.: Sheed, Andrews and McMeel, 1978), p. 2

Chapter 6: Do You Feel Deep Compassion for the Other Person?
[1]Jim Conway, *Men in Mid-Life Crisis* (Elgin, Ill.: David C. Cook, 1978), p. 187.
[2]I don't mean that compassion must be perfect. I've occasionally found that readers are too hard on themselves—too quick to think they do not have adequate compassion when in fact they care for their partner considerably. Compassion should be substantial, but it can never be perfect toward anyone, including the person you marry. Simply because you still

experience selfish episodes doesn't necessarily mean your compassion isn't sufficient. If you feel on the fence about this, consider these questions:

1. Are you willing as a matter of volition to put the other's interests above your own? Are you inclined to do this and able to do it to a reasonable extent? If so, then you meet the most important criterion for compassion. Your considerate behavior toward your partner is even more important than the emotion of compassion, which will always fluctuate.

2. Does your partner believe your compassion is adequate? We are often not good judges of our own positive traits. If the other person feels your compassion is sufficient for marriage, then it probably is.

3. What do others think? Ask several friends or family members whose insight you respect whether they believe your love for your partner is mature enough that they can recommend marriage. Ask the opinion of a professional counselor as well. Take the advice of these people seriously, and give more credence to it than to your own self-judgment.

If you come out positively at these three points, it is likely your compassion is sufficient. If you've been agonizing over whether your compassion is strong enough for marriage, accept as a matter of faith that it is. Focus instead on how your relationship fares in the other areas of compatibility we're considering.

Chapter 7: Are You Good Friends?
[1]Quoted in "How to Stay Married," *Newsweek,* August 24, 1987, p. 54.
[2]Sol Gordon, *Why Love Is Not Enough* (Boston, Mass.: Bob Adams, 1988), p. 38
[3]Ibid., pp. 38-39
[4]Ibid., p. 36.
[5]Larry Richards, *Remarriage: a Healing Gift from God* (Waco, Tex.: Word, 1981), pp. 23-24.

Chapter 8: Are You Both Ready for Marriage?
[1]Maurice Lamm, *The Jewish Way in Love and Marriage* (San Francisco: Harper & Row, 1980), p. 8.
[2]Howard M. Halpern, *Cutting Loose: An Adult Guide to Coming to Terms with Your Parents* (New York: Bantam, 1976).
[3]Since Halpern is not a Christian author, you will not be likely to find his book in a Christian bookstore. In a few places he expresses some perspectives on lifestyle that differ from Christian attitudes. Most of his outlook, though, is quite compatible with Christian thinking, and the book on the whole offers a redemptive and compassionate approach to adult relations with parents. Unfortunately, I don't know of a Christian book to recommend which compares with it.
[4]See for example, Brenda Schaeffer, *Is It Love or Is It Addiction? Falling into Healthy Love* (New York: Harper/Hazelden, 1987); Stanton Peele with Archie Brodsky, *Love and Addiction* (New York: Signet, 1975); Howard M. Halpern, *How to Break Your Addiction to a Person* (Toronto: Bantam, 1982); Connel Cowan and Melvyn Kinder, *Smart Women, Foolish Choices: Finding the Right Men, Avoiding the Wrong Ones* (New York: Signet, 1985); Robin Norwood, *Women Who Love Too Much: When You Keep Wishing and Hoping He'll Change* (New York: Pocket Books, 1985). As with most psychological and self-help books written by non-Christian authors, you will find ideas in each of these that conflict with Christian values. Each book, though, does have valuable insights into the nature of addictive love and practical steps that can help you overcome your vulnerability to unhealthy relationships.

Chapter 11: Are You Spiritually Compatible?
[1]I draw on material here from appendix one of my *Knowing God's Will,* pp. 222-24.

Chapter 12: Are You Emotionally Compatible?

[1]I borrow the term *motivational pattern* from Ralph Mattson and Arthur Miller, who employ it in their books *The Truth about You: Discovering What You Should Be Doing with Your Life* (Old Tappan, N.J.: Revell, 1977) and *Finding a Job You Can Love* (Nashville: Thomas Nelson, 1982), especially chapter six.

[2]Hans Walter Wolff, *Anthropology of the Old Testament* (Philadelphia: Fortress, 1974), pp. 65, 96.

[3]I explore this point in much greater depth and provide many biblical examples in *One of a Kind: A Biblical View of Self-Acceptance* (Downers Grove, Ill.: InterVarsity Press, 1984).

[4]The procedure I recommend here is similar to that recommended in Mattson and Miller, *Finding a Job*, and Richard Nelson Bolles, *What Color Is Your Parachute? A Practical Manual for Job Hunters and Career-Changers* (Berkeley, Calif.: Ten Speed Press, 1984), pp. 83-86.

[5]Paul Tournier, *The Healing of Persons* (New York: Harper & Row, 1965), p. 67.

[6]Keep in mind that these are objective and not judgmental descriptions of personality. *Melancholic*, for instance, doesn't imply melancholy but an analytical and deep-thinking attitude. You will find a thoroughgoing and readable discussion of these four types in O. Hallesby's classic *Temperament and the Christian Faith* (Minneapolis: Augsburg, 1962), which is available in many public libraries. Paul Tournier also has a helpful discussion of them in his *Healing of Persons*, chapter six, also available in public libraries.

Chapter 13: Are Your Expectations Compatible?

[1]Robert L. Mason and Caroline L. Jacobs, *How to Choose the Wrong Marriage Partner and Live Unhappily Ever After* (Atlanta: John Knox Press, 1979), pp. 18-23.

[2]Smith, *Knowing God's Will*, pp. 31-53, 165-72.

Chapter 15: Remarriage

[1]For a thoroughgoing presentation of different Christian viewpoints, see H. Wayne House, ed., *Divorce and Remarriage: Four Christian Views* (Downers Grove, Ill.: InterVarsity Press, 1990).

[2]J. Carl Laney, in ibid., pp. 35-37.

[3]Specific verses where Jesus equates remarriage with adultery are Matthew 5:32; 19:9; Mark 10:11-12; Luke 16:18.

Chapter 18: Understanding the Fear of Commitment

[1]Steven Carter and Julia Sokol document numerous instances of the screeching halt response among men they have known and interviewed in their popular book *Men Who Can't Love: How to Recognize a Commitment-Phobic Man Before He Breaks Your Heart* (New York: Berkeley Books, 1987). While their analysis of the problem is fascinating, they deal only with this extreme level of commitment fear in this book, and they claim it is a serious problem only for men. They have since coauthored another book on commitment anxiety which is much more balanced and comprehensive and offers greater hope for healing: *He's Scared, She's Scared: Understanding the Hidden Fears That Sabotage Your Relationships* (New York: Dell Books, 1995).

[2]M. Blaine Smith, *Overcoming Shyness* (Downers Grove, Ill.: InterVarsity Press, 1993), pp. 73-75, 78-79.

Appendix 1: To Date or Not to Date

[1]Joshua Harris, *I Kissed Dating Goodbye: A New Attitude Toward Romance and Relationships* (Sisters, Ore.: Multnomah Books, 1997); Dr. Don Raunikar, *Choosing God's Best: Wisdom for Lifelong Romance* (Sisters, Ore.: Multnomah Books, 1998).

About the Author

Blaine Smith, a Presbyterian pastor, is director of Nehemiah Ministries, a resource ministry based in the Washington, D.C., area. His work includes giving seminars and lectures, speaking at conferences, counseling and writing. He is author of *Knowing God's Will, The Yes Anxiety, Should I Get Married?, Overcoming Shyness, The Optimism Factor* and *One of a Kind*, as well as numerous articles. He is also lecturer for *Guidance by the Book*, a home study course with audio cassettes produced by the Christian Broadcasting Network as part of their *Living by the Book* series.

Blaine is also a musician and directs the Sons of Thunder, a Christian music ministry, which recently produced a compact disc, *Treasures*.

Blaine is a graduate of Georgetown University and also holds a Master of Divinity from Wesley Theological Seminary and a Doctor of Ministry from Fuller Theological Seminary. He lives in Gaithersburg, Maryland. He and his wife, Evie, have two sons, Benjamin and Nathan, both currently attending college away from home.

You Can Receive Blaine's Newsletter

Blaine authors a monthly newsletter, *Nehemiah Notes*. It lists his activities and always includes an article on a topic related to realizing your potential and staying encouraged in Christ. It is sent for free to anyone requesting it. To request the newsletter or to correspond with Blaine, write:

Nehemiah Ministries
P.O. Box 448
Damascus, MD 20872

On the Internet

Blaine also has an active Internet ministry through a website with Gospel Communications Network, at <www.nehemiahministries.com>. It features information on all of his books, including international versions, plus a twice-monthly posting of *Nehemiah Notes* with numerous articles archived. Most are also available in audio editions.

Nehemiah Notes is also available, free, twice monthly by e-mail. Just drop a request to <nnotes@nehemiahministries.com>.

You may e-mail Blaine personally at <mbs@nehemiahministries.com>.